EXPOSITORY SERMONS
ON THE EPISTLES OF
PETER

EXPOSITORY SERMONS ON THE EPISTLES OF
PETER
W. A. CRISWELL

ZONDERVAN
PUBLISHING HOUSE OF THE ZONDERVAN CORPORATION
GRAND RAPIDS, MICHIGAN 49506

Expository Sermons on the Epistles of Peter
Copyright © 1976 by The Zondervan Corporation
Grand Rapids, Michigan

This printing 1980

Library of Congress Cataloging in Publication Data

Criswell, Wallie A
   Expository sermons on the Epistles of Peter

   1. Bible. N.T. Peter—Sermons.   2. Baptists—Sermons.   3. Sermons, American.   I. Title.
BS2795.4.C74   227'.92'06   76-26486

ISBN 0-310-22811-5

Printed in the United States of America

Dedication

To the young men and women who study God's holy Word
at our Criswell Center for Biblical Studies

CONTENTS

INTRODUCTION

Both congregation and staff at First Baptist Church, Dallas, feel themselves to be uniquely the recipients of our Lord's most gracious mercies. In addition to life and life abundant, God has given to us a pastor-theologian who continually opens to us the rich depths of God's treasury in the biblical revelation. Week after week Dr. W. A. Criswell probes the hearts of members and visitors alike with the deftness of a spiritual surgeon making use of the incisive and revealing scalpel, the Bible. Many drive fifty miles one way, three times a week, in order to hear God speak through this twentieth-century prophet.

I am persuaded that you will discover as you peruse these sermons the rationale which motivates so many of us in the metroplex area to drive past numerous fine suburban churches in order to worship in downtown Dallas. The pastor approaches the preaching assignment with several apparent presuppositions.

(1) The people come to hear a word from God. Therefore, the preacher's task is to enunciate clearly what God has said and relate it to contemporary needs.

(2) The best preaching is expository preaching.

(3) God has promised to honor His Word. Therefore, one may anticipate exciting, life-altering events to occur whenever the Bible is proclaimed.

The sermons in this volume are indicative of a host of others preached in the auditorium of First Baptist Church over thirty-two years and published in more than thirty volumes. On the other hand, these messages are scintillatingly fresh like an oasis in the midst of the sameness of a dry desert of human concerns. Dr. Criswell continues to study laboriously in an effort to proclaim the truth of God effectively to today's generation. The sermons in this volume were preached in Dallas from August, 1973, to July, 1974. They are substantially unchanged from the way in which they were presented to our congregation.

We are delighted to present these biblical messages on 1 and 2 Peter in the tradition of the great preaching of Spurgeon, Truett, and other outstanding evangelicals of yesteryear.

Paige Patterson, President
Criswell Center for Biblical Studies
Dallas, Texas

CHAPTER 1

THE BIG FISHERMAN

1 Peter 1:1

As we begin our study of the Epistles of Peter we begin with Peter's greeting to the chosen of the dispersion. "Peter (*Petros* — rock), an apostle of Jesus Christ to the *diasporas* scattered throughout Pontus, Galatia, Cappadocia, Asia, and Bithynia," provinces in what we know today as Asia Minor. "Elect according to the foreknowledge of God the Father, through sanctification of the Spirit, unto obedience and sprinkling of the blood of Jesus Christ: Grace unto you, and peace, be multiplied." What a beautiful salutation.

PETER'S NAME AND PERSON

In this chapter I would like to have us look at Peter — his name and person. Peter is called "an apostle" — a "sent one" of Jesus Christ. A number of years ago Lloyd Douglas wrote his famous novel entitled *The Big Fisherman*. And the author named that novel correctly, for Peter appears to have been a big man. We have several intimations of that in Scripture. In John 21 we read that the disciples caught a big school of fish. Six of the disciples were wrestling with the full net, trying to get it to land, and we are told that Peter went down and drew the net to shore by himself. That with which six men were struggling, Peter accomplished by himself.

In Acts 3 we read about a man crippled from birth who is is seated at the beautiful gate of the temple asking for alms. Seeing Peter and John, he holds out his hand, expecting to receive alms from them. Peter looks at him and says, "Silver and gold have I none; but such as I have give I thee: In the name of Jesus Christ of Nazareth rise up and walk." Now if you had been born impotent in your feet and had never walked, and if a stranger had passed by and told you to stand up, would you stand up? It would not occur to you that you could, much less that you'd try. So the man just sat there, looking in amazement and wonder at the stranger who told him to get up. He sat with his hand extended, expecting to receive some kind of a pecuniary gift. So Simon Peter took that extended hand and raised the man up. He lifted him up bodily. Look at that! If a man took another man and lifted him under his arms, using his back and shoulders to lift the man up, well, I can see how he could do it. But how does a man reach out and physically raise a person who has never stood in his life? A dead weight — just raised him up with leverage like that. It was a tremendous feat of strength to do that. But that was Simon Peter. He was a big, strong man.

DIFFERENCES IN MEN

In 1 Corinthians 15:41 Paul says that "there is one glory of the sun, and another glory of the moon, and another glory of the stars: for one star differeth from another star in glory." Men in the kingdom are like that. They are different! They are different in affinities and predilections. They are different in personalities and in idiosyncrasies. They are different in temperament, in abilities. The grace of God is not like a steam roller that irons out all the wrinkles of our individualities. We are still ourselves, though serving God. I think of the many preachers I have heard in my lifetime. They are so different. I think of a man like the elder Gypsy Smith. I think of a man like B. B. Crim, the Texas cowboy. They are preaching the same message and yet they are so fundamentally diverse in approach, in thought, and in presentation. There is just one sun, but look at it through stained-glass windows. The same light shines through red, blue, yellow, and green. God's people in His kingdom are like that.

The prophets were like that. Amos was a country preacher. When you read his book you can almost smell the fresh, open forests out in the fields. He talks like a country man. He uses the language and imagery of a farmer. But Isaiah was a court preacher, and we notice his poetic imagery, his chaste and courtly language, yet both men were prophets of God. The same distinction can be made with the apostles of our Lord. Matthew, Thomas, John, and Peter head the list. Peter is no retiring, sweet petunia out in the backyard, wasting his sweetness on the desert. He's heard. He's volatile and impetuous. He is like a mountain stream, rushing down to the valley. He is quick. He is on his feet. He does something and then thinks about it after it is over. For example, when the Lord was washing the disciples' feet He came to Peter to bathe his feet. And Peter said, "Lord, You're not going to wash my feet." And the Lord answered, "Simon, if I don't wash your feet, you have no part with Me." So Peter said, "Then, Lord, wash my hands, my head, and all of me."

IMPETUOUS PETER

As we look at John 18 we see Peter being arrested in the Garden of Gethsemane. The synoptic Gospels do not mention names, but John in his account of the arrest writes, "Simon Peter having a sword drew it, and smote the high priest's servant, and cut off his right ear. The servant's name was Malchus." Cut off his ear. Peter was going to cut off Malchus' head but he ducked, and Peter cut off his right ear. Had he ducked the wrong way Peter would have cleaved him in two. But that is Peter.

Or take the story found in John 21. The eleven were fishing and had caught nothing all night. A "stranger" on shore told them where to cast their nets and John told Peter the man was Jesus. So Peter jumped into the sea and swam to shore. That is Peter.

STRENGTHS AND WEAKNESSES

Now there are three things to notice about men like Peter. First, there is strength in a man like that. Undeniably so. He will strike while the iron is hot. He will act promptly in a moment of danger. He will make a decision in politics or in the marketplace or in business. If he is a general, watching the ebb and flow of battle, he will immediately make a decision. There is strength in a man like that.

We see it in Peter when the Lord came by while Peter and his brother Andrew were fishing on the shores of Galilee and the Lord said to them, "Launch out, and you'll catch fish," and they did. And the rest of the story tells us that the Lord said to Peter, "Come, and follow Me." Peter could have said, "Now, Lord, You are rushing me. Let me think about this. Let me ponder this. Let me turn this over in my mind." Or he could have said, "Now, Master, come back in ten days and call me, or maybe thirty days. You ask me to follow You. Well, after I have had time to consider it and weigh it, then I will give You an answer." The Bible tells us that when the Lord called Peter, he immediately forsook everything and followed Jesus. We see that strength illustrated again at Caesarea Philippi when the Lord asked His apostles who men considered Him to be. They said that some thought him to be John the Baptist raised from the dead, some felt He was Elijah, and some that He was the weeping prophet Jeremiah or one of the other prophets. Then the Lord asked, "Whom do you say that I am?" We can almost see those apostles pondering the question in their minds. And it was Peter who spoke up. He said, "Thou art the

Christ, the Son of the living God." He made that affirmation without
fear of contradiction. There is strength in a man like that. It reminds
us of Martin Luther standing before the Diet of Worms. "Here I
stand. I can do no other, so help me God." There is strength in a man
like that. You cannot help but be impressed with such a confidence in
this day of anything goes, when you are taught that you are not
supposed to have any convictions. So we weigh the arguments on this
side and we weigh the arguments on the other side and we never
come to any convictions. It just may be that we do not actually believe
anything.

When I was a boy there was a column in the daily newspaper
entitled "Today," and it was written by a man named Arthur Brisbain. I remember reading in one column that Mr. Brisbain mentioned he was no religionist. He was no follower of God or Christ, but
he always went to hear Billy Sunday preach. One day a man discussed
this with him and Mr. Brisbain wrote about it in his column. The man
said, "It is strange that you go to hear Billy Sunday. Why Billy Sunday
believes in a devil that wears a red suit, has a forked tail, and has a
pitchfork in his hand with which he stokes the fires. It is unthinkable.
Why do you go to hear Billy Sunday when you do not believe
anything he says?" And Arthur Brisbain answered, "I just like to hear
him because he believes it." There is strength in that man. He stands
up and says what he believes. He knows his own mind and he avows
it. He has conviction, and you feel it. Did the Lord say blessed are
those who are always discussing, philosophizing, and speculating?
No. Blessed are they who do the will of God. They shall enter into the
kingdom of heaven.

We have discussed the strengths in a man like Peter but there are
also weaknesses in a man like him. He is like a pendulum, A man like
that tends to go to extremes. He is over on one side and then he goes
to an extreme on the other side. The Lord told His apostles that all of
them were going to forsake Him — all of them. And the spokesman of
the apostles, Simon Peter, said, "Now, Lord, all of these other eleven
may forsake You, but I won't." "Simon, you will not forsake Me?"
"No, Lord. I will lay down my life for You. I will follow You to death. I
will not forsake You." Then the Lord said, "Simon, I say to you that
before the cock crows twice you will deny me three times." Oh, the
vacillation of a man like that.

Let us look at Peter in another situation as it is recorded in Acts 10
and 11. God used a vision of a sheet let down from heaven full of all
kinds of unclean creatures to inform Peter he was to go to the house of
a Gentile named Cornelius. When Peter went into the house of

Cornelius he told the many there that it was a tradition that a Jew was not to enter the house of a Gentile and he certainly was not to stay there and break bread with him. But God taught Peter that we are not to call any man common or unclean. Jesus had died for all men. So Peter broke the old barrier and we see him with Gentiles, eating, drinking, and fellowshiping with them.

In Galatians 2 Paul tells us that Peter came down to Antioch, and when certain representatives came from James, Peter played the hypocrite. In Acts 10 and 11 we read of Peter breaking every barrier and every racial tradition by eating with the Gentiles, and in Galatians 2 we read of him withdrawing himself and dissimulating. Therefore Paul said he had to confront him "to the face." Peter was a strange mixture of cowardice and courage, of rugged strength and instability. He was always striking 12:00 — either 12:00 at the high noon hour in some marvelous triumph or he was striking 12:00 at the midnight hour in some dismal failure. He was never at 9:00 in the morning or 3:00 in the afternoon. He was always up or he was always down. It was one or the other with him.

GOD'S USE OF A MAN LIKE PETER

The third thing we can say about a man like Peter is that God has a use for him. The Lord found in that volatile spirit of Peter a man who was teachable. After the catch of many fish, Peter fell at the feet of Jesus and said to Him, "Depart from me; for I am a sinful man." At the close of John 6, after the Lord had delivered His sermon on the bread of life and after everyone had left Him, He turned to the disciples and asked, "Will ye also go away?" Simon then said, "Lord, to whom shall we go?" There is no one else to go to. They were staying with the Lord. After the Lord taught Peter the way, the truth, and the life, Peter knew there was nowhere else to go. What a great lesson Peter learned. Oh, Peter still would sway. Satan still would try to ruin Peter, and Jesus knew this. He told Peter the devil would try to sift him like wheat, but the Lord was praying for him.

When the soldiers arrested the Lord, Peter ran like a coward; and as he warmed himself by the fire, while the Lord was being tried before the Sanhedrin, a little maid accused him of being a follower of Jesus, and Peter denied it. He also let out a stream of cursing. The Lord knew what Peter had done and we are told He "looked" at Peter. And that look hurt. The Bible says Peter went out across the road and wept bitterly. He was that kind of a man, but the Lord was not done with him. And when we do things like that, are you not glad He is not done with us? God has a great vision and has a great purpose for us. He has plans for us. And He never looks at our worst but always looks at our best. It is not what we are but what we can be. When the Lord was raised from the dead, He told the women at the tomb to tell "my disciples and Peter."

In John 21, after breakfast along the shore, Christ turned to Peter and said, "Feed My little ones, My lambs." God was not done with Peter. In Acts 4 we read that the leaders of the city of Jerusalem saw the boldness, the lion-roaring of Peter, and all because he had been with Jesus. You would not have thought it a short time earlier. He is called "Petros" — a rock. Jesus saw it in him. Jesus looks at us like that. He sees what we can be and, with His grace, will be.

The following poem was written by a black man, and it has the imagery of a typical black preacher. The poem is about Jesus looking at Peter. He sees him made of sand, and he is unstable. He needs something. So this black poet calls it cement, which is the Holy Spirit, and He takes the cement, the sand, and the water, and He makes out of it a rock.

Dear Lor — (That Jesus bless God our Savior)
De Lord see his ciples and he sat and think
He's de men I don called to de word.
Matthew and Tholemu, James and John
and every last one of them heard.
There's Andrew and Philip and Thomas and Jude
and each is a pendable man, but Peter is the one
I call out fist and Peter is like the shifting sand.
Peter blow dis way and Peter blow dat way.
Oh!!! What I do wid Peter?
Matthew is my staff what I cut from the oak.
I leans on him at my will.
Philip is my arrow, shooting straight from the bow.
James is the candle on a hill.
John is my lamp that they can't blow out, shinin'
just as steady as can be.
But Peter is the one I count on most and Peter is
like the changing sea.
Peter moves dis way — Peter move dat way.
Oh!!! What I gonna do wid Peter?
Oh, what a gwana do wid sand and water? Both of
them slipping away.
When dey's mixed like in Peter you can mold and
shape, but how you gwana make it stay?
Dey needs cement. Dat's the spirit of the Lawd. And
notin' else can hold him fast.
Ifn it's poured in the sand and water now maybe
Peter gwine to last. Oh, de sand
and the water don make the rock. Dat's what I don wid Peter.

Isn't that something? That is the marvelous thing about the Lord. He sees us now, as we are, but He also sees what we can be. He sees us at our best.

ALWAYS IN GOD'S MIND

A sculptor sees an angel in solid rock before he chisels it out. An artist sees a beautiful painting before he puts it on a canvas. An architect sees a magnificent building in his mind before he draws up the plans. Jesus is like that. He sees us at our best. He encourages us. He lifts us up. When we are discouraged He does not add to our burden and frustration. He has words of comfort. He believes in us. I cannot think of a better title for a sermon to preach that "God Is for Us." What a blessedness.

CHAPTER 2

SAFE IN GOD

1 Peter 1:1-5

In 1 Peter, the first chapter, we now consider the first five verses. "Peter, an apostle of Jesus Christ, to the strangers scattered throughout Pontus, Galatia, Cappadocia, Asia, and Bithynia, Elect according to the foreknowledge of God the Father, through sanctification of the Spirit, unto obedience and sprinkling of the blood of Jesus Christ: Grace unto you, and peace, be multiplied. Blessed be the God and Father of our Lord Jesus Christ, which according to his abundant mercy hath begotten us again unto a lively hope by the resurrection of Jesus Christ from the dead, To an inheritance incorruptible, and undefiled, and that fadeth not away, reserved in heaven for you, Who are kept by the power of God through faith unto salvation ready to be revealed in the last time."

CALLED TO BE SAVED

"Peter, an apostle of Jesus Christ, to the strangers — to the *diaspora.*" The *diaspora* refers to the scattering of the Jews after the destruction of Jerusalem, the temple, and the Judean state. It refers to the scattering of the Jewish people over the earth, and the apostle Peter uses it here to refer to the scattering abroad of the believers in Christ. It designates the Jewish people who had accepted Christ as their Savior. Pontus, Galatia, Cappadocia, Asia, and Bithynia were Roman provinces in what we now know as Asia Minor. Peter was well able to direct an epistle to them because for more than thirty years he had been an emissary for Jesus Christ, preaching among those people the blessed gospel of our Lord. There is no fragment of evidence that Peter was ever in Rome. We can follow the life of Peter through every day that he lived until he was crucified, and we shall find that he was always in the east. So he addresses his letter to the people he knew in

Pontus, Galatia, Cappadocia, Asia, and Bithynia — the great mass of
the eastern portion of the ancient Roman empire. Now he speaks to
them: "Elect according to the foreknowledge of God the Father,
through sanctification of the Spirit, unto obedience and sprinkling of
the blood of Jesus Christ."

Notice that Peter believes in the trinity. "Elect according to the
foreknowledge of God . . . of the Spirit . . . and . . . of Jesus Christ."
He is a trinitarian, just as we are today. And he speaks of those of the
diaspora as being *eklektos*, from which we have our word "elect."
They are the chosen — *eklektos*. We are God's chosen because of His
prognosis, and it is spelled the same way we spell it in English.
According to the *prognosis* — *pro gnosis* — according to the foreknowledge of God. There is nothing that surprises the Lord. Always
remember that. Nor is there anything that happens except under His
divine sovereignty. Satan does not run this universe. He may think
he does, but all the issues of time and life ultimately are in the hands
of almighty God and are according to the *prognosis* — the foreknowledge of God Himself. He wrote our names in the Book of Life
before the foundation of the earth. We are the elect according to the
foreknowledge of God.

GRACE AND PEACE

Then Peter addresses his readers with both a Greek and a Hebrew
word of salutation. The Greek word is *charis* — grace. Our name
Karen comes from this and many girls today are named Karen. Grace
unto you and *shalom*. Few people today are not familiar with that
Hebrew word *shalom*. The word means peace and in Greek it is
spelled *eirene*. If you have a daughter named Irene that is the Greek
spelling of the word for peace. So the Greek and Hebrew greeting
means "grace and peace to you."

Peter continues, "Blessed be the God and Father of our Lord Jesus
Christ, which according to his abundant mercy hath begotten us
again unto a [living] hope by the resurrection of Jesus Christ from the
dead." He wants us to believe that we are saved — begotten again —
born again by the mercy of God as Paul wrote in Titus 3:5, "Not by
works of righteousness which we have done, but according to his
mercy he saved us." We are saved not because we were worthy, nor
because we did good, nor because we merited God's favor, but
because of the abounding mercy of God. When I get to thinking about
that, I wonder how I can praise His name enough that He chose me.
Why was I not born a Hottentot in the heart of Africa? Why was I not
born an Australian aborigine? How is it that I was born in a Christian

home? How is it that I heard the gospel of Christ, that I was saved, begotten again by the Holy Spirit? I praise His name according to the mercy of God that I was born into the kingdom of our Savior. When we're born the first time we are born with a body, with breath, with mind, and with heart. But when we are born again, we are born into the glorious riches of the gifts of God in His blessed kingdom.

We are born again "unto a [living] hope by the resurrection of Jesus Christ from the dead." Look at that a moment. We are born again into a living hope by the resurrection of Jesus from the dead. And we are going to see what that same experience obtains for us today. There was a time when Peter believed that the kingdom of God was going to be an earthly, messianic empire. And he thought he was going to have a worthy and significant place in that earthly kingdom. Maybe he would be prime minister or maybe he would be chancellor. The mother of Zebedee had asked that her sons, John and James, could sit one at Christ's right hand and the other at His left hand. Peter thought of a messianic kingdom in terms of a great world empire. Jesus would be king and He would be a marvelous leader in that earthly and glorious domain. But then the crucifixion of Christ crushed that hope. When Peter saw Jesus arrested and crucified in shame on that cross, every hope he had was dashed to the ground. Not only that, but his own personal defection and denial ruined him. He was crushed with added sorrow to think that he would curse and deny his Lord. The One from whom tears might have brought forgiveness was dead and buried. We cannot imagine what that meant to the apostles. How high their hopes were and these hopes of an earthly messianic kingdom were hopelessly lost when they saw Jesus dying. Peter experienced this frustration, and that is why he said that God has begotten us again unto a living hope by the resurrection of Jesus Christ from the dead. When Jesus was raised from the dead He told the women to tell His apostles — and Peter. Again, we cannot imagine the exultation in the heart of that apostle when he saw Jesus raised from the dead, when Jesus talked to him and forgave him. Imagine his joy when Christ mandated him to the glorious work to which God had called him. All of this was possible because of the raising of Jesus Christ from the dead.

Christians, that is our experience, too. The apostle Paul writes of us in Ephesians 2:1 when he says that all of us were dead in trespasses and in sins, and in verse 12 he says we were without God in the world and had no hope. A lost man is like that: he is without hope. All that lies ahead of him is death and beyond that is the horror of a judgment. But when we are born again, we are begotten again unto a living hope by the resurrection of Jesus Christ from the dead; for the gospel tells us that when Jesus died we died with Him, and when Jesus was raised from the dead we were raised with Him.

That's why we are baptized. Baptism signifies that we are dead with Christ. We die to sinful self and our sins are deeply buried. When we were raised in those baptismal waters, we also were raised with Him.

Let me illustrate this from the story of Goliath and David. Goliath represented the uncircumcised Philistine who blasphemed and damned the name of God, and no one dared challenge him. All of God's people cringed in fear. Then came the champion David. He represented God, and he represented every hope of the chosen family. When Goliath fell and was slain by David, that represented the triumph of the people of God. Goliath came before David with a sword and a shield, but David came in the name of the Lord God whom Goliath had defied. When David slew Goliath he was our representative, and that is exactly what the resurrection of Christ has done for us. The Lord died for our sins. He was buried and our sins were buried with Him. When He was raised from the dead He was raised for our justification, to declare us righteous in the presence of God. He is our representative, and we have been born again unto our living hope by the resurrection of Jesus Christ from the dead. That is why we sing about Him — to glorify God in the resurrection. That is why in the household of faith there is always that uplifting note, no matter how dark, how sad, or how full of despair any situation may be. That is why in the household of God there is always in it that note of a better tomorrow. Jesus still reigns on the throne.

KEPT BY GOD'S POWER

Furthermore, God's people are "kept by the power of God through faith unto salvation ready to be revealed *apocalupto* in the last time." Did you ever hear that word *apocalupto* before? Turn to verse 7 of this same chapter and read that we "might be found unto praise and honour and glory at the appearing [*apocalupsis*] of Jesus Christ." In verse 13 we read, "Wherefore gird up the loins of your mind, be sober, and hope to the end for the grace that is to be brought unto you at the revelation [*apocalupsis*] of Jesus Christ." Three times in this chapter Peter mentions the fact that we also have *apocalupses*, an uncovering, ready to be revealed at the last time. We are to share in all the glories that are in Christ — every one of them. We are fellow heirs with Him. When you read of all the glories of God from the *apocalupsis,* they are your glories too. If there is glory for the Son, there is glory for His joint heirs. If Christ is triumphant, we are triumphant. If He comes into a kingdom, we shall come into a kingdom. If He is reigning, we shall reign. If He is exalted, we shall be exalted. If He is Lord of all the earth, we also shall sit on thrones.

Can you conceive of what God has done for us, and that we can place our trust in Him? Respond to Him with your life.

CHAPTER 3

LOVING THE UNSEEN CHRIST

1 Peter 1:6-9

Let us take a look at verse 8. "Whom having not seen, ye love; in whom, though now ye see him not, yet believing, ye rejoice with joy unspeakable and full of glory." Notice the pronoun Peter uses: "Whom having not seen, *ye* love." Peter could not use "we" because he had seen the Lord. From the days of John the Baptist, at which time Peter was baptized, all through the years of His public ministry, Christ had by His side this chief apostle. So Peter could not say "whom having not seen, *we* love," but "whom having not seen, *ye* love," for we have not seen the Lord in the flesh.

THE PRIVILEGE OF SEEING CHRIST

In Matthew 13 our Lord told His disciples that "many prophets and righteous men have desired to see those things which ye see, and have not seen them; and to hear those things which ye hear and have not heard them." How blessed are the eyes of the disciples. Oh, the privilege of having seen the Lord. An old divine once said there were three things he wished he could have seen — Rome in her glory, Paul preaching at Athens, and Jesus in the flesh. One of the incomparable prophecies of the new heaven, the new earth, and the new Jerusalem is this: in the midst of the city, the river of life, and the tree of life, will be found the throne of God and of the Lamb. And we shall see His face. Think of it, we shall look upon the face of Jesus Christ in rapture, adoration, and worship. It is because of the desire of our soul to see the Lord, that for centuries artists have employed every ingenuity at their command and every concept imaginable to paint a picture of the Lord. They have tried to show us how He looked. Yet, after all their vain attempts there is not one of those paintings that somehow does not tell you that man has not yet achieved a portrayal of the glorious personality of the Son of God. It is impossible to capture. For that reason when I read or hear about scoffers and infidels who mock the miracles of our Lord, I say in my heart that there is no man who lives who could say what might or might not happen in the presence of Jesus Christ, the Son of God. And it is that inability to capture Him which makes it impossible to portray His face. What did He look like? To me it is an amazing fact that in all of Scripture there is no hint of how the Savior actually looked — His hands, the color of His eyes and His hair, His stature, the form of His face, and the fashion of His body. Evidently the Lord had a reason for not giving us a physical picture. It is best we do not know.

SEEING CHRIST IN THE FLESH ONLY

The apostle Paul wrote a strange sentence in 2 Corinthians 5:16: "Though we have known Christ after the flesh, yet now henceforth know we him no more." Whether Paul meant that though he had seen the Lord in the flesh, yet he was not preaching a physical Christ, I do not know. I have always supposed that Paul first looked upon Jesus when the Lord appeared to him on the Damascus Road. Regardless of that to which the sentence refers, certainly the preaching of the apostle is that we are not to bow physically before a flesh-and-blood Christ. Our worship is to be a spiritual revelation that it might not be revealed to us how Jesus looked in the flesh.

If I were to speculate, I might think that one reason God hid the actual appearance of Christ from our eyes is because of our sensuality. We so easily drift into that. Do you remember Luke 11? A crowd was surrounding Jesus; and a woman in the crowd, seeing the marvelous power in the man of God, lifted up her voice and said, "Blessed is the womb that bare thee, and the paps which thou hast sucked." Is that not something unusual to exclaim in an audience? It shows you how easy it is to become sensual in our response. Or consider the disciples before the Lord went to heaven and before Pentecost. They constantly looked for and planned for a physical Judean kingdom. And when the Lord on the top of Mount Olivet was ready to go back to heaven, they asked Him, "Lord, wilt thou at this time restore again the kingdom to Israel? One of us is planning to be prime minister and another is planning to be secretary of the treasury, and You are getting ready to leave us. Where is that physical, earthly Israelite kingdom?" It is so easy for us to drift into those thoughts and to leave out the deep spiritual relationships and entities we know in God. Though there is no revelation of the actual physical appearance of the Lord Jesus, nor is there any hint of it, this does not mean we are estranged from Him. The apostle says that though we have not seen Him, His face has never been beheld by us, yet we are joined to Him in a deep relationship of love and faith. "Whom having not seen, ye love; in whom, though now ye see him not, yet believing, ye rejoice with joy unspeakable and full of glory."

THE JOY OF SEEING CHRIST

The verse speaks of faith and love, and they link us in an intimate relationship with our blessed Lord. Where one is, the other follows hard after. They are inextricably interwoven, and are twin celestial sisters of the soul. And they join us to our Savior. We become Christians by believing, by faith that Christ might dwell in our hearts. The Lord said to the doubting apostle, "Thomas, because thou hast seen me, thou hast believed; blessed are they [*makarioi*, happy are they] that have not seen, and yet have believed." This is a beatitude for all of us who look in faith to Jesus. "Blessed are they that have not seen, and yet have believed." How precious. And the apostle Paul, speaking of the eternity, said that we look not at the things that are seen, but at the things that are not seen, for the things that are seen are temporal, but the things that are not seen are eternal. The great author of Hebrews in the 11th chapter says, "By faith Moses . . . endured, as seeing him who is invisible." He comes to us gloriously by faith, and not by sight.

One of the most unusual of all prefaces to a book is that written by Erasmus in the Textus Receptus, the first Greek New Testament, printed in 1515. Erasmus wrote these words: "These holy pages (talking about the Greek New Testament) will summon the living image of His mind. They will give you Christ Himself, talking, healing, dying, rising, the whole Christ in a word. They will give Him to you in an intimacy so close that He would be less visible to you if He stood before your very eyes." What an amazing statement. Christ is revealed to us in the Word of God more fully, more gloriously, more intimately than if He stood in our presence and we looked at Him with our naked eyes. Joy unto Christ by faith and joy unto Him by love. The Christian faith is Christ, and our response is devotion to and love for the Lord; that makes us Christians. It is Christ.

Let me illustrate. You can have Confucianism without Confucius. If you just gather together all the maxims of ancient Chinese culture you can have what appears to be Confucianism. You can have Hinduism without their sages and their mahatmas. You can have Christian Science without Mary Baker Glover Patterson Eddy. You don't need any of them, but you can't have Christianity without Christ. The Christian faith is our Lord. And it is love for our Lord that makes it ours. The apostle Paul wrote, "For we preach not ourselves, but

Christ Jesus the Lord; and ourselves your servants for Jesus' sake."

A preacher was quoting 2 Timothy 1:12, "For I know in whom I have believed, and am persuaded that he is able to keep that which I've committed unto him against that day." Right in the middle of the sermon an elderly saint stood up and said, "Sir, don't put a preposition between me and my Lord. Not 'I know in whom I have believed,' but 'I know whom I have believed.'" That is the faith and that is the love that joins us to God; and without that all-consuming love in our hearts for Jesus, we cannot be Christian.

LOVING THE UNSEEN CHRIST

In 1 Corinthians 16 the apostle by inspiration wrote, "If any man love not the Lord Jesus Christ, let him be Anathema." It is our love for Christ that makes us Christians. Sometimes that love can be expressed in adoring silence — just being quiet in His presence. Sometimes that love can be expressed by irrepressible tears like showers of rain — tears falling from our faces in His presence. Sometimes that love can be expressed by deeds of mercy done in His name. Sometimes that love is expressed by the confession of His faith at the peril of life. However, it may be that it will always express itself if you love the Lord. In fact, that is the heart of the Christian faith. The Lord Himself said, "This is the first and great commandment: thou shalt love the Lord thy God with all thy heart, and with all thy soul, and with all thy mind." Thus when someone comes along and sarcastically speaks of the cheapness of emotion in religion, I cannot fully understand for the very fountain springs of life are in our emotions.

I recently read a psychology book in which the thesis of the author was that the fountain springs of life are our emotions. And he discussed them: love, hate, jealousy, fear, ambition, and on and on. It is likewise so in religion. Take feeling or emotion out of religion and it turns to dust and ashes in our hands. Think of a person's patriotism or love of country. Man was born with an emotion or feeling for the country of his birth. So we are bound to our Lord by emotions, by love. The apostle writes "whom having not seen, ye love; in whom, though now ye see him not, yet believing, ye rejoice with joy unspeakable and full of glory." What joy unspeakable! If you lived in the days when you were put in prison because you couldn't pay your debts and a man came and told you he had paid them, would you not rejoice? Or if you were facing inevitable death and were not prepared to die, least of all to face God at the judgment, would you not rejoice if someone would justify you, speak words of righteousness and forgiveness to you? That is the joy of our text. "Rejoice with joy unspeakable and full of glory." We have a little bit of heaven here. We have a foretaste of the river of life. We can almost hear the angel chorus. We somehow taste the grapes gathered from the vineyard of the Promised Land. And we have a few flowers from the pastures of paradise, full of glory. We have just a little picture of the immortality and the glory that is yet to be.

THE UNSEEN CHRIST AND OUR TRIALS

Let us now look at the context in which our text is written. We must remember that this epistle was written to the scattered Christians of "Pontus, Galatia, Cappadocia, Asia, and Bithynia" and these Christians were in the midst of a great trial of affliction. You know the story of how Nero was supposed to have fiddled while Rome burned. The populace accused him of setting the city on fire and pointed a finger at him. In order to divert suspicion from himself Nero accused the despised Christians. So in the golden city of Rome the Christians were persecuted, and the provinces, taking their cue from the capital city, persecuted them even more. Thus the Christians in Asia Minor, as we know the area today, were undergoing a great trial. But the apostle writes to them and says, "Wherein ye greatly rejoice, though now for a season, the trial of your faith is much more precious than gold." Isn't that an astonishing thing to say?

Just what is Peter saying? He is telling the Christians they can rejoice in their trials because they are God's elect. We are elect according to the foreknowledge of God. Before the Lord laid the foundations of the world He saw us and knew us, and He wrote our names in the Book of Life. They stand there forever. Do I believe that? I do. Do I believe in election? I do. Do I believe in foreknowledge? I do. Do I believe in predestination? I do. I think God is not surprised or overwhelmed by anything that happens in this world. We are the elect according to the sovereign grace of God before the foundations of the earth were laid. And I rejoice in this truth. I am elected through the sanctification of the Spirit and the sprinkling of the blood of Jesus. I am clothed with the righteousness of the Lord. My heart is sprinkled with the blood of Jesus and that cleanses all my sin and stain. How I rejoice in that beautiful truth! I am elected to an inheritance incorruptible and undefiled, that does not fade away, and is reserved in heaven for me. "On Jordan's stormy banks I stand, and cast a wishful eye to Canaan's fair and happy land, where my possessions lie." There, not here. If our possessions were here, we would have to leave them, but they are ours in heaven.

Therefore we can rejoice, we "who are kept by the power of God through faith unto salvation ready to be revealed in the last time." The Lord Jesus said it beautifully in John 10:28,29, "I give unto them eternal life; and they shall never perish. . . . My Father, which gave them me, is greater than all; and no man is able to pluck them out of my Father's hand."

Can I believe that? Let us take it to the Lord and ask Him about it. Lord, You say that we are kept by the power of God unto salvation. You say that You give to us eternal life and we will never perish. But, God, I may yet stumble into hell. I may fall into the abyss. I may go along in this Christian life until the last week or the last day or the last hour and then miss it. Let me ask You, Lord, if You were down here where we are and if You knew our life of suffering and our hurt, and if the way is hard and the trials are heavy, and our faith would begin to fail and we would begin to murmur, would we not perish? At that moment we hear "I give unto them eternal life; they shall *never perish.*"

But, Lord, what if the hurt becomes unbearable, and what if we turn aside and doubt whether You hear or whether You answer prayer and we are miserable, then would we perish? And the Lord replies, "I give to you eternal life and you will never perish." But, God, what if the pain was so great and the trial so heavy, and I lost my senses, and in the losing of my mind in the hurt, I said something that would pervert my faith? Would I be lost? The Lord says, "I give unto you eternal life and you will never perish — never." You are kept by the power of God.

> The soul that on Jesus hath leaned for repose
> I will not, I will not desert to his foes.
> That soul though all hell should endeavor to shake,
> I'll never, no, never, no, never forsake.

"Fear not, little flock; for it is your Father's good pleasure to give you the kingdom."

> Sometimes on the mount where the sun shines so bright,
> God leads His dear children along;
> Sometimes in the valley, in darkest of night
> God leads His dear children along.
> Some through the waters, some through the flood,
> Some through the fire, but all through the blood;
> Some through great sorrow, but God gives a song,
> In the night season and all the day long.

"Kept by the power of God, wherein ye greatly rejoice." Oh, bless His wonderful name.

CHAPTER 4

WITNESSES TO CHRIST

1 Peter 1:10-12

In our last chapter we discussed the fact that even though we have not seen Christ in the flesh, we still can rejoice with joy unspeakable and full of glory. Verse 9 mentions the salvation of our souls, which is the consummation of our faith, and Peter writes the words of our text: "Of which salvation the prophets have inquired and searched diligently, who prophesied of the grace that should come unto you: Searching what, or what manner of time the Spirit of Christ which was in them did signify, when it testified beforehand the sufferings of Christ, and the glory that should follow. Unto whom it was revealed, that not unto themselves, but unto us they did minister the things, which are now reported unto you by them that have preached the gospel unto you with the Holy Ghost sent down from heaven; which things the angels desire to look into."

The Message of the Gospel

Our text consists of long and involved sentences, but they have infinite meaning and significance for us. Peter speaks of those who witness to the gospel of Jesus Christ, and he names first the prophets. By the Spirit of Christ that was in them they testified beforehand of the sufferings of Christ and the glory that should follow. The salvation is the same, the message is the same, the gospel is the same. The Old Testament and the New Testament are one book. They were inspired by the same Spirit and their subject matter is the same subject matter. Old and New alike point to Christ, the Son of God. The messenger may change, but the message is always the same. Whether the gospel is preached by a prophet who foreviews it, or declared by an apostle who looks back to it, the message is the same. Whether it is Isaiah, who describes the sufferings of Christ 750 years

29

before they take place, or an apostle, such as Paul, who describes the message of Calvary 30 years after Christ, the message is always the same. Whether it is the prophet Daniel who is writing down his apocalyptic visions, or the sainted John who is delineating the consummation of the age, the revelation is always the same.

Let me illustrate. The gospel message the Bible presents has always been one of grace. It is without cost or price. It is a free gift, and whether that message is presented by a prophet or by an apostle, it is always the same. Isaiah speaks of it like this: "Ho, every one that thirsteth, come ye to the waters . . . Yea, come, buy wine and milk without money and without price. Wherefore do ye spend money for that which is not bread? and your labour for that which satisfieth not? hearken . . . incline your ear . . . and your soul shall live."

Now listen to the same message of grace as it is preached by the apostle Paul. "For by grace are ye saved through faith; and that not of yourselves: it is the gift of God; not of works, lest any man should boast." Man cannot say "I did it." It is something God bestows upon us without money and without price. Whether Isaiah preaches or Paul proclaims, it is the same salvation in the same way.

The message of salvation is presented as one of faith. The channel through which it is extended to us and by which we receive it is one of faith. Whether it is in the Old Testament or the New Testament, it is always the same. Moses wrote of it like this: "Abraham believed God, and it was accounted to him for righteousness." The apostle Paul preached it like this: "But to him that worketh not, but believeth on him that justifieth the ungodly, his faith is counted for righteousness" (Rom. 4:5). Whether spoken by Moses in the Old Testament or by the apostle Paul in the New Testament, the message is always the same. Look again in the Old Testament. We are told that we are saved by looking to God, and in the New Testament the same gospel says we are to look and live. Isaiah, quoting the Lord Jehovah in heaven, said, "Look unto me, and be ye saved, all the ends of the earth: for I am God, and there is none else" (45:22). The apostle John, writing of our Lord, said it like this: "As Moses lifted up the serpent in the wilderness, even so must the Son of man be lifted up: that whosoever believeth in him should not perish, but have eternal life" (John 3:14,15). Whether it is by Isaiah or by the apostle John, the message is the same. It is this: look and live, believe and be saved.

> I've a message from the Lord, Hallelujah!
> The message unto you I'll give;
> 'Tis recorded in His word, Hallelujah!
> It is only that you look and live.

THE BLESSINGS OF THE GOSPEL

The message is always the same on any page of the Bible. By the voice of any prophet or apostle, the salvation is ever the same. That is why the first four books of the New Testament are called Gospels. They are the *euangelion*. They contain the good news of God — and that by inspiration. I think the early Christians called those four narratives by Matthew, Mark, Luke, and John the four Gospels. That was the message and the revelation toward which all the prophets looked, and it was the message of the good news that every prophecy which the apostles preached to the people had been fulfilled in Him. It is the gospel message of salvation that never changes. If our Lord Jesus is preaching the Sermon on the Mount, it is the gospel of kingdom citizenship. If our Lord is working miracles, the miracles are the gospel of hope and of faith. As we stand before the awesome mysteries of disease and death, the tears of Jesus are the gospel of the compassion and sympathy of our heavenly Father. The blessedness of the ministries of our Lord in His love for the people is the gospel of God's sympathy and understanding with human error and human weakness. The death of Christ on the cross is the gospel of His suffering — in the travail of His soul and for His sake, God was satisfied, and for His sake forgave our sins. The resurrection of Jesus Christ from the dead is the gospel that assures our ultimate victory and triumph. Always it is the central revelation that God placed into the hearts of the prophets by foreview and into the hearts of the apostles in their proclamation. Our Lord died for our sins according to the Scriptures, according to the prophecies of the prophets, and the third day He was raised again according to the Scriptures, as the prophets had foreseen it. He was received up into glory and is set down on the right hand of the majesty on high. The prophets spoke of the sufferings of Christ and the glory that should follow. Our humanity is exalted to the throne of deity itself. And He — the King of the universe — is there not by popular decision, but by divine right. All authority had been committed to Him in heaven and in earth. His power is unspent. Though we do not now see our Lord reigning over God's creation, yet by the prophetic foreview and by the revelation given to the apostles, someday He will reign as King over all God's creation.

This is the message unchanging. Peter says of the prophets that they inquired and searched diligently what manner of message it was that the Spirit of Christ in them was delivering to the people. That the prophet himself searched and inquired diligently into the meaning of the message he bore is unusual. You have that expressed in 2 Peter 1:21, "For the prophecy came not in old time by the will of man"; it was not a human speculation. It was not a knowledgeable judgment. The prophet did not consider the times and weigh the evidences and give a human judgment, but the prophecy came in old time and not by the will of man. It was not something that came out of his human discernment, but men of God spoke as they were moved by the Holy Spirit. What the prophet wrote down was what the Spirit of God moved him to say and to write, and most of the time the prophet did not fully understand the word that was delivered to him. Thus he inquired and searched diligently into it.

THE LANGUAGE OF THE GOSPEL

We have poignant examples of the leading of the Holy Spirit in the writing of the Old Testament. The prophet Daniel says, "I heard but I did not understand." He wrote down the message the angel delivered to him, but he said, "I heard the words and I wrote them down. I saw the vision, but I didn't understand it." That amazing conjuncture of time and eternity, of travail and triumph, of life and death, of suffering and salvation was revealed to the prophet but he said he didn't understand it.

Look again at Isaiah, the prince of the prophets, the court preacher in the days of the kings of Judah. In one breath the prophet Isaiah, in language beautiful beyond any poetry the world has ever heard, writes; "For unto us a child is born, unto us a son is given: and the government shall be upon his shoulder: and his name shall be called Wonderful, Counsellor, The mighty God, The everlasting Father, The Prince of Peace. Of the increase of his government and peace there shall be no end, upon the throne of David, and upon his kingdom, to order it, and to establish it with justice from henceforth even for ever. . . . The wolf also shall dwell with the lamb, and the leopard shall lie down with the kid; and the calf and the young lion and the fatling together; and a little child shall lead them . . . the lion shall eat straw like the ox . . . They shall not hurt nor destroy in all my holy mountain: for the earth shall be full of the knowledge of the LORD, as the waters cover the sea" (9:6,7; 11:6-9).

What amazing statements, and when we hear them how do we receive them? "Who hath believed our report? and to whom is the arm of the Lord revealed? For he shall grow up before him as a tender plant, and as a root out of a dry ground: he hath no form nor comeliness; and when we shall see him, there is no beauty that we should desire him. He is despised and rejected of men; a man of sorrows, and acquainted with grief: and we hid as it were our faces from him; he was despised, and we esteemed him not. Surely he hath borne our griefs, and carried our sorrows: yet we did esteem him stricken, smitten of God, and afflicted. But he was wounded for our transgressions, he was bruised for our iniquities: the chastisement of our peace was upon him; and with his stripes we are healed. All we like sheep have gone astray; we have turned every one to his own way; and the Lord hath laid on him the iniquity of us all" (Isa. 53:1-6).

How did Isaiah put all those prophecies together? I'm sure he didn't understand it all. The apostle Peter says the prophet spake, moved by the Holy Spirit of God, and into the message revealed to him he inquired and searched diligently.

WITNESSES TO THE GOSPEL

John the Baptist had the same problem. According to Christ, though John was the greatest of prophets, even this forerunner of our Lord could not understand. One time during his ministry John sent a messenger to the Lord asking Him if He was the coming one, the great prince of glory, the king of the universe. "Is it You or do we look for someone else? When the prophet speaks of the suffering servant and the humble one, could that be You? Then when the prophet speaks of the glorious and shining and reigning one, is that another Christ?" John did not understand. We do understand. Christ came the first time to wear a crown of thorns. He is coming the second time to wear the crown of all creation. We understand it now, but the prophet didn't. Peter indicated that though they did not minister to themselves, not having understood, they have ministered to us, who are are in turn preaching the gospel with the power of the Holy Spirit. In other words, the prophet did not understand it, but in delivering his message faithfully he ministered to us, who now can see that the prophetic message of the Old Testament confirms and corroborates that the child Jesus is the Son of God. The gospel message is verified and authenticated because it was preached by Isaiah 750 years earlier, it was preached by Moses 1,400 years earlier, it was preached by Abraham 2,000 years earlier, and thousands of years before that God revealed it to Adam and Eve in the Garden of Eden. And what they have said ministers to us now. We have authentication beyond dispute that this is the truth of God. Not only does the prophet witness to the grace of God in the Lord Jesus Christ, but he furthermore ministers with the help of the Holy Ghost sent down from heaven.

The apostles were witnesses to the truth as well as to the saving grace and power of the Son of God. They proclaimed in a military world the grace and the forgiveness of Jesus Christ. Oh, how effective they were. They had no other robes except those of poverty. They had no other distinctiveness except shame and suffering. They had no other power but the weapon of the presence of the Holy Spirit. But how faithfully they delivered their message. They evangelized in the homes of the people, in the rural areas, the country and the villages, finally to the cities and even to Caesar's household. There the apostles faithfully brought the message of the truth of the cross of the Son of God and finally bore that message far away to the heathen of the known world. The very word for "witness" in the Greek New Testament is *martus*. So often did the Christian witness pay for his faith with his own death that the word carried over into our English language as a transliteration of *martus* — i.e., martyr, signifying one who lays down his life for the faith. How glorious is the testimony of the witnesses to the truth of God in Christ Jesus. Peter says the Holy Spirit is sent down from heaven and these witnesses preach the gospel in the power of the Spirit of God from heaven. It was the Holy Spirit who empowered the prophet to see. It was the Holy Spirit who fell upon Jesus to do. It was the Holy Spirit who came upon the apostles in their preaching and it is the Holy Spirit who empowers us today and works with us today. There is no possibility of revealing the fullness and the glory of the gospel of Christ apart from the Holy Spirit of God. Nor is there any possibility of a man being converted and saved except in the unction and saving power of the same third member of the trinitarian godhead. We can keep the gospel to ourselves, but the heathen remain the same unless the gospel is borne in the power and on the wings of the Holy Spirit to the human heart. Without Him there is no conversion. The heathen may hear the words; but unless they are empowered by the convicting presence of the Holy Spirit of God, they will not be converted. It was the Holy Spirit who worked with Christ in the days of His ministry. First, at His baptism the Holy Spirit had to come upon Him as He began His messianic ministry. The apostles likewise were told to wait in Jerusalem until they were endowed with power from on high. That same blessedness must come upon us in heavenly grace if we are to be used of God to reach the human heart and to convert the human soul today.

Let me illustrate. Recently I read of a pioneer preacher who was successful in converting the frontiersmen. What kind of a man was he? He was uneducated and he spoke in coarse grammar and in rude language. His library was a Bible and a hymn book. Often his message was mixed with error. But he pressed across the Alleghenies, and into the wilderness of Kentucky and Tennessee and through the broad prairies of Ohio, Indiana, and Illinois. He pressed westward preaching under an arbor, under trees, in log cabins. Wherever men would gather together, there he preached the gospel of the Son of God. He pressed to the west and eventually reached the waters of the Pacific. Such men — though uneducated, coarse, crude, and unacceptable in any modern, cultured pulpit in America — such men turned this continent to Christ and established many of the churches and institutions that now bless our homes and hearts. The Holy Spirit worked with them and God used them to turn America to Christ. Today many leaders in the Christian theological world are highly educated. They write learned tomes and speak in deep and recondite nomenclature. In the pulpit they snore theology and the people listen while sound asleep. They have emptied the churches of Europe and are beginning with the churches of America.

As president of the Southern Baptist convention I was presiding at a meeting in Nashville, Tennessee. A large convocation of our Baptist leaders was at a dinner and Billy Graham was the speaker. I can still remember his saying that he could not understand why a people would embrace a theology that had emptied the churches of continental Europe. I don't understand it either. The theology of a Barth, of a Bultmann, and of a Bonhoeffer is dead. Such nothingness does not have in it the moving, convicting Spirit of the saving power of God. I cannot help but compare these men with our coarse frontiersmen who preached the message of Christ in a language that was ungrammatical and rough, but the Spirit of God in their hearts witnessed with them and the people who listened were saved. The churches were founded and organized and the institutions were lost. Today Barth's successors can speak in learned, academic, theological language but without power. When we have no Christ, we have no message. When we have no Spirit, we have no power.

> Come Holy Spirit, heavenly dove, With all Thy quickening powers, Kindle a flame of sacred love in these cold hearts of ours.

Oh, blessed God work with us! Help us! Take the words we say and the message we bring, and empower it to move, to convict, to convert the hearts of the people.

ANGELS AND THE GOSPEL

I would like to discuss one other clause, "which things the angels desire to look into." The angels were astonished at the sufferings of Christ and the glory that should follow after. Is it not surprising that the angels wanted to inquire into the sufferings and glory of Christ? If I were to say to you, "Come, here is a door that opens into heaven, let us look in that door," would we not all eagerly gather around the door to look at the vistas of glory? Just imagine what you would see. Look at those gates made out of solid pearl. Look at those foundations — all of pure gem. Look at that jasper wall. I think jasper is a word in the New Testament for "diamond," so the wall is made out of solid diamond. I found out recently that one carat of some diamonds can cost $20,000 a carat. That's hardly a speck in the walls made out of solid, pure, white diamond. Would you not like to see something like that? And would you not be amazed as you look at the golden streets? Gold is now so high that one little American gold coin costs you $200. It is so plentiful in heaven that you can use it for paving. And look at the throne — look at the water of life — look at the tree of life — and look at God's redeemed. When I think of standing there, I can hardly take it all in.

But the apostle says the angels crowd around the windows of heaven and look down at us. They are amazed and filled with desire to understand as they see Christ dying for our sins, raised for our justification, and the Spirit of God wooing and convicting the human heart. They are looking down on us, and they are filled with wonder and amazement at what they see. They are like the two angels — the cherubim — with their wings overspread, looking down upon the mercy seat. They gaze at it in awe and reverence. The Bible tells us there is joy in the presence of the angels of God because of one sinner who repents. They look down and are overwhelmed by the grace they see flowing from the wounds of Christ, the salvation that pours from His heart, the blessedness of His cross and the winning of a soul. What a blessedness! What a glory! What a wonderment! And it is ours for the taking!

CHAPTER 5

THE COMING OF CHRIST

1 Peter 1:13

"Wherefore gird up the loins of your mind, be sober, and hope to the end for the grace that is to be brought unto you at the revelation of Jesus Christ." What a thought — at the *apocalupsis* of Jesus Christ. The Book of Revelation begins with that word, and it is a significant word full of meaning. In the days of Christ's earthly walk, His humanity covered Him. Just once in a while did His deity shine through, such as on the Mount of Transfiguration when His face became as the sun in its strength and His raiment as white as the snow. Now He is hidden from sight, waiting until the earth is made His footstool and all His enemies are subject to His name. But there is coming a time of unveiling when the Lord will appear in all His deity and glory.

THE LORD IS COMING SOON

It is remarkable when you read these pages from the apostles how full their minds were of the Lord. They were steeped in the things of Jesus and one of the things that was constantly before them was the return, the revelation of Jesus Christ. The apostle Peter, for example, says in the seventh verse of this chapter "that the trial of your faith . . . might be found unto praise and honour and glory at the appearing of Jesus Christ." And our text speaks of the grace that shall be brought to us at the revelation of Jesus Christ. Peter tells us in his second letter that he did not follow cunningly devised fables when he made known to us the power and visible presence of the Lord. And the entire third chapter of 2 Peter is given to a description of the consummation of the end time when the Lord shall come again. The apostles believed in the imminency, the nearness of the coming of Christ. Were they mistaken? No, for they were dealing in eternities and the ages between are but as a moment.

Another thing, they looked upon the event with indescribable joy and anticipation. In 2 Peter 3 Peter says that the whole creation will be on fire and that the elements will melt with fervent heat, but they were not afraid of the dissolution of the world and the consummation of the age, for to them that meant that Jesus was coming. The Bridegroom of their souls was drawing nigh, and they used the revelation of the coming of our Lord as a motive for obedience, purity, holiness, and faithful work for the Lord. Our text says, "Wherefore gird up the loins of your mind, be sober, and hope to the end for the grace that is to be brought unto you at the revelation of Jesus Christ; as obedient children." There could hardly be a finer motive for Christian work and devotion than this: the Lord is coming soon. We are His stewards, and when He comes, we must be found ready and waiting.

THE LORD IS COMING FOR HIS OWN

So the apostle begins our text with a "wherefore." This word and "therefore" are common words for the apostles. They are used often by Peter. He begins the second chapter with the word. In the sixth verse of that chapter he says "wherefore" and in the seventh verse he uses "therefore." As I read from these holy men I discover that true religion is rational and reasonable, bringing our faculties and perceptions up to their highest heavenly usefulness. True religion is neither far out, nor is it fanatical. Rather it commands the finest thought and the highest honor from the greatest minds in the human race. "Wherefore" implies it is a rational faith that we have embraced — one which appeals to a sound mind.

What does Peter mean when he says, "Wherefore gird up the loins of your mind, be sober, and hope for the grace that is to be brought unto you at the *apocalupsis* of Jesus Christ"? The "wherefore" refers to what he has said before. He has already noted that we are the elect according to the foreknowledge of God and according to the sprinkling of the blood of Jesus Christ. We have been washed clean and white in the blood of the Lamb. "Wherefore" refers to the fact that we have been elected to an inheritance incorruptible, undefiled, that does not fade away and is reserved in heaven for us. Ours is the harp of gold and the starry crown, and we will see the King in His beauty and will share the rulership of the entire universe with our joint heir — Jesus Christ. "Wherefore" refers to Peter's statement that we are the elect and are kept by the power of God. There is a wall of fire that surrounds the people of the Lord and not until the immortal God can die will the least of the Lord's saints be lost. We are kept by the power of God. Peter continues by saying that we are tried in our faith to praise, honor, and glory at the *apocalupsis* of Jesus Christ. Our trial does not work for us some evil thing but through our pilgrimage in this world it is to bring us honor and glory under God. Abraham's trial of faith won for him the crown as the father of the faithful. Our Lord's trial and suffering brought His love to us as the Savior, and our trial and temptation in this life brings us to God in honor and in glory. The word "wherefore" refers to the joy we will have when we see the Lord, "whom having not seen, ye love; in whom, though now ye see him not, yet believing, ye rejoice with joy unspeakable and full of glory."

WE MUST BE READY

The Christian has two heavens — he has one *here* with the Lord and he has one *there* with the Lord. Whether here or there, he is one with the Lord, and the "wherefore" refers to those marvelous endowments and gifts the Lord has brought to us in His grace and love. Thus the apostle says, "Gird up the loins of your mind." What magnificent imagery! To many people, religion seems to hang on them loosely as though it didn't fit or as if it is about to fall off. To so many of us the faith of Christ is something like quicksilver — when you touch it, it breaks apart. Paul says we are to cover up the loins of our minds. I wonder why the apostle used that figure — "gird up." I wonder if it comes from his own mannerism. For example, three times in John 21 we read of Peter girding himself. He girded his fisher's coat about him and came to Jesus. In verse 18 the Lord talks to him, reminding him that in his youth he could gird himself and go where he wanted, but in his old age he would need another to gird him. Girding might be a mannerism peculiar to Peter. I wonder if it might refer in imagery to what happened at the Passover when the Lord said that each person there was to have his staff in his hand and his loins girded, ready to march for his Lord. I wonder if it might refer to the happiness and the joy God's people have when, overflowing in gratitude to Him, they gird up their loins like Elijah and run all the way from Mount Carmel to Jezreel. We run and are not weary, we walk and do not faint. However the imagery may have been peculiar to Peter, the habit of girding is apparent in the use of the metaphor. The clothing of the easterner was long and flowing, and if he went into battle or if he ran a race, he had to gather his clothing around him and tie it up tight with a girdle or a belt, lest the flowing robes entangle his feet and cause him to fall. So, the apostle says, we are to gird up the loins of our minds as though we were getting ready for a warfare or for a race. Our experience confirms that it is easy to drift downstream, but if we go against the current we toil in rowing. Following the inclinations of the world would be easy, but mounting the steep ascent to heaven requires effort. We must gird up for the race or for the fight. Our Lord emphasized that truth when talking about John the Baptist. He said, "From the days of John the Baptist until now the kingdom of heaven suffereth violence, and the violent take it by force." The soft and the easy do not win heaven. It is received by dedication. It is a warfare in Christ.

John Bunyan describes the pilgrim life in beautiful imagery when he unfolds the entrance into heaven. He pictures heaven at the top of a great staircase and there is warfare on every step. As the pilgrim mounts and ascends upward he sees singers on the top of the staircase, welcoming the pilgrim in with much joy and glory. However, many struggle to enter into the beautiful city but are thrust away because the gate is blocked by men who fight against those who would enter. Bunyan says that looking, he sees a man come with determination written on his countenance. The man walks up to the one at the gate and tells him to record his name. When his name is recorded, the man draws out his sword, ascends the steps, and fearfully combats those blocking the way. A great fight ensues, but the man conquers and makes a lane through those who hindered the progress of the Christian pilgrim, and he enters in triumph, conquest, and glory.

Now that is a poet's description of what it is to gain heaven, but he is not far wrong; for the Christian life is an obedient life. It is a dedicated life. It is a sacrificial life, and heaven is won by those who give themselves to the will and purposes of God. We are therefore to gird up the loins of our minds — be sober — we are not to be distracted and distraught, but we are to have calm, clear minds. Could I say this means we are not to listen to those who shout the loudest on the streets, nor to those who beat the biggest drum, but we are to be confidently and quietly assured of the promises of God? We are to gird up the loins of our minds, and hope to the end. In times of great trial or sadness or discouragement when circumstances can overwhelm us — we are prone to lose hope. Even God seems to have forgotten us. Sometimes God seems to be against Himself. Abraham must have wondered at times. God told him that all the nations of the world would be blessed through him. The blessing was to come through Isaac, not Ishmael. Then the Lord came to Abraham and told him to take his son Isaac and go to the top of Mount Moriah. He was then to take Isaac, bind him, build an altar, place Isaac on the altar, take a knife, plunge it into his heart, and offer him as a sacrifice.

What was Abraham to do? What do you do when promise seems to be against promise and when God seems to be against God and you do not understand? You hope to the end. You never lose faith. You never give up. The New Testament says that Abraham did not stagger at the promises of God but believed that God was able to raise Isaac from the dead. Rather than have God break His word or have His promise prove untrue, Abraham prepared to sacrifice his son, believing that the Lord would raise him from the dead.

Ah, the hope, the faith that never fails. Therefore we should gird up the loins of our minds and wait for the grace that is to be brought to us at the appearing of Jesus Christ. Notice the phrase, "for the grace that is to be brought" to us. The grace is not in us. There is no personal merit. When a man stands before God in his own righteousness, he is clothed in filthy rags. If Abraham had to be justified by his works, he would never have seen the glory. God knew him just as God knows you and me; and when we stand in His presence, our personal pride and our vain self-esteem turn to dust and ashes because He knows all about us. There is not one of us who can stand before God in his own strength, his own purity, his own righteousness, his own goodness. We just are not righteous. The Lord deals with us in grace. He did it from the beginning and He has never failed.

What is the grace we are waiting for at the coming of the Lord? Is it atoning grace? No. For that was brought to us in the first advent of the Lord Jesus, when He died to wash our sins away. The day of atonement brings afresh to our minds and souls what Christ did for us on a hill called Calvary. Is it justification then? No, for the Lord gave that to us when He was raised from the dead to declare us righteous. Justification means to declare someone righteous. A person is justified before the throne of God when Christ declares us righteous by His resurrection from the dead. He had the right to do it, and He does it. He is at the right hand of the throne of God now interceding for us who by faith come to Him.

FINAL AND FULL SALVATION

If it is not atoning grace and if it is not justifying grace, then surely this grace that shall come at the return of the Lord must be sanctifying grace. No, for sanctifying grace was poured out upon us at Pentecost when the Spirit was given. Then what kind of grace is this that the Lord shall bring to us at His coming? We find that grace in the words of our text. Peter speaks of the faith God gave us when we were saved — ready to be revealed at the last time. The grace that God will bring to us at the last time will be the final and full salvation. Now we see

God's redemptive work in part, just a little of it. It is something like an earnest. When we accepted the Lord as our Savior, we trusted in Him and He saved us. He regenerated our hearts, He gave us a new love, a new vision, a new hope, a new promise, and a new tomorrow. But the full purchased possession is yet to be won. Our full salvation will not be ours until the appearing of Jesus Christ.

As long as I live in this body of death I will have the drag of my old carnal nature. I continue to do what I do not want to do and I do not do what I should, but when the Lord comes and that full redemption will be mine, this old carnality will be taken away. There will be no more of the drag of weakness and sin in my life. I will be delivered wholly and completely. Not only that, I will have the whole purchased possession — a new, glorified, and immortalized body. If you live long enough you will know about the daily struggle, the suffering and weariness, and you may even live long enough for your mind to decay. Of all the sadnesses of life I know of nothing more sad than to see someone who used to be so strong but is now cut down so that the mind does not function properly anymore. No wonder Paul said that if in this life only we have hope in Christ we are of all men most miserable. That is why Peter speaks of the glorious fullness of salvation at the unveiling of Jesus Christ, and he speaks of the vindication of our faith at the appearing of Christ. The world is full of scoffers and mockers who think we are soft in our heads, that we need crutches to walk this life because we speak of religion. They feel adequate in themselves — they do not need any crutches such as religion. They do not need anyone to pray to unless they pray to themselves. They do not need any strength outside their own abilities and adequacies, and they look upon us who bow before Jesus as weak. The apostle says that our faith will be vindicated at the coming of the Lord. When the mists have rolled away all perplexities that somehow frustrate and beset us will be saved. When the Lord comes, He will have answers for them all and the trust we have placed in the blessed Jesus will prove to be the sweetest, the most precious of all the possessions we have had in this world. When everything else has passed away, there shall remain our love for our Lord and His personal appearing.

THE GLORY OF HEAVEN

Now just a word about the glory that shall follow. What is glory? And what is the glory that shall follow? I presume you may have many definitions for it, but as I read the Holy Scriptures, Christ in you is the hope of glory. To me, glory is the manifestation of God in us, the shining of the Lord in us. We shall reflect the image of God. I grant you that sometimes we do not reflect much of the beauty and holiness of the Lord Jesus now, but there is coming a time when each one of God's saints will reflect the image and the glory of his Savior. Oh, happy day, wonderful day, glorious day. It is the day the apostles spoke of so often, the day Jesus promised so faithfully, and in which we believe so devoutly — it is the unveiling, the coming of the Lord. What a day that will be!

CHAPTER 6

THE BLOOD OF CHRIST

1 Peter 1:18-20

We now come to a precious passage in our study of the Epistles of Peter. The verses are 1:18-20. Verse 18 begins, "Forasmuch as ye know that ye were not redeemed with corruptible things, as silver and gold, from your vain conversation." The Greek word for conversation is *anastrophēs*, which means manner of life, behavior, the way you used to live. Peter says the believer now is redeemed "with the precious blood of Christ as of a lamb without blemish and without spot: who verily was foreordained before the foundation of the world, but was manifest in these last times for you." We are redeemed, brought back to God, not with corruptible things — not with worldly things as silver and gold — perishable things, but with the precious, *timio*, blood of Christ. The word *timiō* refers to something of incomparable cost.

It is easy to fall into the habit of preaching about the gospel, but not the gospel itself. However, when we speak on and expound a text like ours we are brought back to the heart of the gospel message of Christ. This is one way of discovering whether the message is of God or of men. In so many areas of the modern liberal Christian world the preaching of the blood is offensive. I have been in churches where hymns on the blood have been purged from all the hymn books, and the liberal theologian looks upon a text such as ours as a religion of the butcher shop. But the presentation of the whole revelation of God in the Scriptures is ever the same — there is no remission of sins without the shedding of blood, and from the beginning in Genesis to the Book of Revelation the whole gospel story is that Christ is come into the world to die for our sins according to the Scriptures. We are redeemed not with earthly things, corruptible things, but with the precious blood of Jesus Christ. In the Scriptures God looks upon blood always as being *timiō*, precious. Even the blood of animals is precious in His sight.

THE SHEDDING OF BLOOD

In Genesis 9 God says that man is not to eat flesh with blood in it because life is in the blood. Blood is precious to God; it is given on the altar as an atonement for our souls. In the Mosaic legislation the people were prohibited from eating things strangled because the blood was still in the flesh. The blood was used upon the altar, poured out at the base of the altar for an atonement for our sins. The life of the flesh is in the blood, and "I have given it to you upon the altar to make an atonement for your souls: for it is the blood that maketh an atonement for the soul" (Lev. 17:11). And when the Lord looked upon the crimson of life poured out, even though it was that of a bullock or of a lamb, yet in God's sight it was precious. The blood of man is even more precious in His sight. In Genesis 9 God says that if a man's life is taken the person who took his life must pay for it with his own blood (v. 6). And in the Book of Numbers God says the shedding of blood by violence, by murder, defiles the land (35:33). It cries to God as the blood of Abel cried to the Lord of heaven.

THE BLOOD OF CHRIST

If the blood of animals and the blood of men is precious to God, what shall we say about the blood of God's Son, our redeeming Savior? In Acts 20:28 the apostle Paul says that our church was purchased by the blood of God. That is an amazing and astonishing expression. In the work for my doctorate I took a course on the atonement. It was one of my minors. We studied the atonement for two years, and at the end of the course I had to take an oral examination. I can tell you that at the end of those two years of graduate study on the atonement, I felt I understood less of the mysteries of the atonement than when I began. If there is anything that defies description it is the atoning death of Christ. How does the blood wash away our sins? And what are the sufferings of Christ into which we can hardly enter?

> But none of the ransomed ever knew how deep were the waters crossed,
> Nor how dark was the night that the Lord went through ere He found His sheep that was lost.

As I read this text I am ready to confess that my finite mind cannot enter into the mysteries of the atoning grace of God in Jesus Christ, but as I study the Bible and pray over its pages, there are some things that come to my heart about the blood of our Lord.

THE BLOOD OF CHRIST AND ATONING GRACE

First, the blood of Christ brings to us God's atoning grace. The law says "this do and thou shalt live." We are to obey this commandment and we will have eternal life. But how does a man keep the law of God, and how can he learn to be perfect in all his ways, when his every effort is characterized by mistake and sin? So the man brings for his sin a sacrifice. He comes before God with a bullock, but has to come again and again. So his life is one of a perpetual memory of his sin and shortcomings. The high priest goes into the Holy of Holies with blood of expiation and he returns again. There is no end. What does the blood of Christ do for us? The apostle Paul writes in Romans 10:4, "For Christ is the end of the law for righteousness to every one that believeth." In Romans 5:9 he tells us that we are now "justified by his blood, we shall be saved from wrath through him." Christ is the end of the law. If we look in faith to Him, His blood will redeem us from the wrath and judgment of God upon our sins. Outside of Christ we are slaves to the tyrant of the law. The law threatens us, curses us, and judges us. There is no righteous man before the law. All have sinned and come short of the expectation of God. What does a man do, therefore, who finds himself always a sinner? The blood of Christ brings to him the grace of God. Under the shelter of God's love, mercy, and grace the judgments have been placated.

In the tabernacle sanctuary is found the ark of the covenant. In that ark we find the Ten Commandments, written on tables of stone. How many of them do we break every day? The judgments of God are upon our sin, but to the one who has trusted in Christ, his sins are covered by the sprinkled blood of atonement, grace, and forgiveness. Our Lord was the victim; He was slain and His blood poured out in order that we need no longer fear the judgments and penalty of our sin. How was this done? By things earthly, things such as silver and gold? No, we were redeemed by the precious blood of Christ by a spiritual intervention of God from heaven. I do not deny that silver and gold can redeem some things. If a man in great need of money pawns a diamond or anything else that is precious, he can buy it back with gold or silver. There are some things that corruptible things can redeem. If a man places his home under mortgage, he can buy back the mortgage. But how can you redeem a destroyed soul and how can you redeem a ruined life with gold and silver? It cannot be done, yet we try to do it. We try to further ourselves by affluence. We try to commend ourselves to God by our own righteousnesses and we think for the most part that if a man has money, if he has gold, silver, stocks and bonds, he has become secure. The man will say it was all because of his possessions. But God says it is by His grace. The man says with money and with price — God says without money and without price. The man looks on the pages of Dun & Bradstreet, but God says we are to look through the pages of the Lamb's Book of Life. God does not look for stocks, bonds, lands, or possessions. He looks for the blood, and when a man is saved, he is saved by being under the blood.

> What can wash away my sin? Nothing but the blood of Jesus;
> What can make me whole again? Nothing but the blood of Jesus.
> Oh! precious is the flow That makes me white as snow;
> No other fount I know, Nothing but the blood of Jesus.

What does the blood of Jesus do for us? It brings to us God's atoning grace.

THE BLOOD OF CHRIST AND THE WASHING OF SINS

We now come to the second truth: it is in the blood of Christ that our sins are washed away. We are not saved by His miraculous birth, nor by His beautiful life, nor by His miracles that could change the course of nature. Not even by His words of wisdom, though never man spake like this man, but we are saved by the blood of the cross. And the death of Christ is not exemplary. He did not die to teach us an example. He did not die for our inspiration, but He died for our sins according to the Scriptures. What God seeks in us is a response of humility, repentance, and acceptance so that through the blood of the Son of God we might be cleansed, we might be acceptable in His sight. And this is no accident in history, nor is it something ephemeral or peripheral in the plan of God, for the prophet says that the spilling of the precious blood of Christ was foreordained before the foundation of the world, before God flung the stars and the planets into space, and before He created this earth. Christ died for our sins according to the foreknowledge and sovereign elective grace of God. It is in the blood of Christ that we are justified. It is in the blood of Christ that the church is born. It is in the blood of Christ that we have hope of forgiveness for sins. And by the blood of Christ He has quenched all the altar fires on the earth. It is difficult for us in this modern day to realize that in the day of the Egyptian, the Babylonian, the Assyrian, and of the Greek and the Roman that the entire earth was covered with altars and the smoke of fires ascending up to heaven. As far as I know there is not one altar burning in the earth today. Why? The atoning grace of God in Christ Jesus quenched all the altar fires on the earth. There are no more priestly orders, for He is our High Priest, making intercession for us in the sanctuary of God. Our Lord was obedient to the law for us in His life. In death He paid the penalty of sin for us. In His death He was the scapegoat that carried away the sins of His people. In the Resurrection He not only was declared to be the Son of God but He also brought justification to declare us righteous in His presence when He comes again. In His return He will bring to us a complete salvation. It will be the complete redemption of the purchased possession, a resurrected immortalized body as well as a redeemed and blood-bought soul.

The Blood of Christ and Regeneration

What has the blood of Jesus Christ done for us? It has brought to us not only God's grace and forgiveness for our sins, but the blood of Christ also brings to us the promise and the power of a glorious, redeemed, and regenerated life. It is a marvelous thing that in the poured-out blood of our Lord we have the poured-out blessings of God and of heaven upon us. The life of our Lord literally was poured out into this world and that love and grace comes even to us. When the soldiers smote the Son of God, they struck the rock from which flows the living waters. When they pierced His hands and His feet, they opened the resources of grace and power and glory from heaven, and when they pierced His side, they opened the fountain of God's love, and grace, and mercy. Not only that, but in that gift of God's love in the life of His Son, there came with it that cleansing, regenerating power that makes us new men and women, new creations in God's sight.

Recently I spoke to a national convocation in Arlington, Virginia. It was a meeting of prison chaplains and the people who support them. I was surprised at the beauty of the occasion. It was convened in a beautiful hall, and there were present about 600 men and women who were resplendently dressed. I was seated at the speaker's table, sitting at the side of the executive leader of the group. He proceeded to tell me about every person at our table plus many others. He seemed to know all about them. While he was talking to me, I was reminded of the Auca Indians of Peru. For many years they had bathed their hands in human blood but later had been won to Christ. I went to preach to them one time and found them faithful disciples of our blessed Jesus.

At the convocation in Arlington I listened in amazement to many of the speakers. The one was as fine looking a man as you could ever see. The director sitting next to me told me he was the chairman of their board. He had been convicted years earlier of embezzling in a bank, sent to prison for a long sentence, but in prison the grace of God found his heart and changed his life. Now he is not only a fine businessman, but he also is a deacon in his church and the treasurer of the congregation. Another man had been convicted time and again, for he had written more than $40,000 in bogus checks. He now is a fine leader and officer in a national corporation. Another speaker had been a murderer and had been sent to the penitentiary for shedding man's blood. But in prison God's grace changed his heart and life and the governor had bestowed upon him a full pardon.

Let me continue. Another speaker was a former hit man for the Mafia — a man who who is hired to kill other men. This man was sentenced to life in the penitentiary. But the grace of God reached his heart, cleansed his soul, and he, too, had been given a full pardon by the government. Still another speaker — and he really touched my heart — had become deranged over a tragedy that overwhelmed the world in the Second World War. You may remember the Nuremberg Trials in Germany for the Nazi war criminals. There were four men from four different nations assigned to carry out the execution and this man was the American representative. He himself had hanged twenty-two men, and he said that as the days passed the oppression of the assignment unbalanced his mind and he turned to alcohol and finally to drugs. Because of this he was sent to the penitentiary, but through a prison chaplain the Lord Jesus Christ healed his mind and his soul and made him a new man. Now he is a stalwart defender of the faith.

I think of another man who was sentenced to forty years in prison. This man has not only been pardoned — he also is a great Christian, and speaks to groups all over the eastern part of the United States, warning young men in schools and colleges of the terror of the evil way of life and sharing the blessings and glory of life in Christ. As I listened to testimonies of the marvelous grace of God that had come down from heaven in Christ, I could hardly imagine how such a thing could be. I thought of the marvelous, incomparable, indescribable blessings that God has shed upon us, has poured out upon us in the atoning grace of our blessed Lord — the precious blood that buys us, redeems us from judgment.

THE BLOOD OF CHRIST FOR ME

Have you ever noticed how we categorize sins? Do you see that man over there — he is a violent sinner. Do you see that one over there — he's the dregs of the earth. And do you see this one here? He is as dirt and filth. We have a tendency to gather our righteous skirts around us and talk about how sinful other people are. Then we remember the word of the Lord, in which God says all have sinned — all. There is not one of us who is righteous — no, not one. One man may have sinned in one category and another in a different category, but I also have sinned in my categories. My life is full of blemish and wrong and I need to be saved just as the next person does. I also need to cast myself upon the mercies of God. I too need to say, "Lord, be merciful to me, a sinner." And, praise God, the same loving grace that was extended to others is extended to me. Under the blood we all are saved. "When I see the blood I will pass over you." There is no more condemnation to those who are in Christ Jesus. We are free. We are washed. We are redeemed. We are justified by the blood of the crucified One. I come openly, unashamedly, confessing my faith in the Son of glory.

CHAPTER 7

FOUNDATION FOR THE FAITH

1 Peter 1:23-25

"Being born again, not of corruptible seed, but of incorruptible, by the word of God, which liveth and abideth for ever. For all flesh is as grass, and all the glory of man as the flower of grass. The grass withereth, and the flower thereof falleth away: but the word of the Lord endureth for ever. And this is the word which by the gospel is preached unto you." You can easily see why I love this text. In the heart of it the apostle quotes from Isaiah 40:8, which is my favorite verse in the Bible: "The grass withereth, the flower fadeth: but the word of our God shall stand for ever." Peter says something in our text that is astonishing. "Being born again . . . by the word of God, which liveth and abideth for ever." Can such a thing be? We are born again. We are regenerated. We are made members of the family of God by the Word of God that is preached. We are born again by the Word of God, "and this is the word which by the gospel is preached unto you." It is astonishing that Peter could write such a thing. But lest we think that such a presentation is unique, all we need do is look at the Bible and see the witness of the Word itself. We will find that throughout the Word of the Lord this thought is stated again and again.

Let us turn to James, the epistle written by our Lord's brother. We read in James 1:18, "Of his own will begat he us with the word of truth." We are born into the kingdom of God by the word of His will. Lest we think that unusual, the apostle Paul wrote in Ephesians 5:26 that we are cleansed "with the washing of water by the word." It is the Word of God that purifies us, cleanses us, regenerates us, presents us blameless and faultless in His holy presence. We can illustrate this further. Our Lord Jesus Himself says to His disciples in John 15:3: "Now ye are clean through the word which I have spoken unto you."

So you see, we are born again by the Word of God. To me this is the meaning of the message of our Lord to Nicodemus, teacher of Israel, when He said to him in the third chapter of John, "Except a man be born of water and of the Spirit, he cannot enter into the kingdom of God." A man must be born of water, of the cleansing of the sanctifying power of the Word of God. The witness of the testimony of the Holy Scriptures to itself is astonishing — born again by the Word of God, and this is the Word by which the gospel is preached to you. Would that not be defense enough and encouragement enough for a man to preach the Bible?

This chapter is a discussion of the importance and necessity of the Word in the saving of souls. The apostles have written about it and Jesus has spoken of it. There is no ultimate reality except as it is revealed to us in the Word of God, as it is revealed to us in the Holy Scriptures. You cannot know, you will never know, except as God reveals it.

THE WORD AND GOD

We know God only as He discloses Himself, reveals Himself in His holy Word. There is no possibility of a man knowing God apart from the Word of the revelation. A man by searching cannot find God. I can look into the starry firmament forever and be impressed. Whoever made those stars must have been someone of infinite power. But what is His name and who is He? I could never know just by searching. Or, I can look at a beautiful sunset or a colorful rainbow or at the blue of the sky or at the green of the waters and I could think that God loved beautiful things. What purpose is a sunset? What utilitarian reason lies back of a rainbow, or why the blue of the sky? God just loved it that way. But who is He who did it? And what is His name? I could never know. Or I can see the great tides of the sea. Or I could see the power of a hurricane or a cyclone and conclude that the great Maker of this universe is one of power, but who is He? What is His name? I could look inside me and find that I am sensitive to good and evil, and I could conclude that whoever made me is also someone who knows right from wrong. But what is His name? I could never know except as He reveals Himself. If I am to know God, it must come through a self-disclosure of the Almighty in the holy Word.

THE WORD AND JESUS

I could never know Jesus except as He is revealed in the Word. Apart from one or two exceptions there is no record of Christ in secular history. One of the first-century Latin historians, Suetonius, in describing Nero's persecutions of the Christians, felt obliged to describe the Christians. He says that the Christians were named after one Christ who was executed as a felon under Pontius Pilate, the Roman procurator of Judea. And outside of that little historical reference, there is no record of Jesus at all. Even the paragraph in Josephus that names the Lord is spurious according to scholars. You would never know Jesus except as He is revealed to us in the Bible.

THE WORD AND SALVATION

Also, we would never know how to be saved apart from reading the way in the Word of God. We would never be able to find the gate to heaven except as God has revealed it to us in the Book. Do you remember how John Bunyan begins his pilgrim's progress? It starts like this: "As I walked through the wilderness of this world, I lighted on a certain place where was a den, and laid me down in that place to sleep; and as I slept, I dreamed a dream. I dreamed, and behold, I saw a man clothed with rags, standing in a certain place, with a face from his own house, a book in his hand, and a great burden upon his back. I looked, and saw him open the book, and read therein; and as he read, he wept and trembled; and, not being able longer to contain, he broke out with a lamentable cry, saying, 'What shall I do?'" Bunyan continues the story and describes the man as looking this way and that way as if he would flee. He did not know where to turn, so he just stood still. Then a man named Evangelist pointed out to the pilgrim a little wicket gate and beyond that a hill called Calvary and on the top of the hill a cross. Evangelist told the pilgrim that if he would go through that wicket gate he would find at the cross the burden of his sins rolled away, and he would receive hope and salvation and the promise of life. It just does not work that way. There is no finding that little wicket gate. There is no coming to God in salvation except as the Lord reveals it to us in His blessed Book.

THE WORD AND THE WILL OF GOD

And we could never know the will of God for us if the Lord had not written it and revealed it to us in the Bible. What is it God wants of us? How can a man obey God and follow in His way? One of the greatest joys a pastor can experience is to see his people more and more seeking God's will from the pages of His Book. It is not advantageous — it is purposive. It is not incidental — it is central and dynamic. God's people must increasingly be rooted and grounded in the faith presented on the sacred pages. What God has written there we see everywhere. The church must be busy seeking to do what God says in the Word.

Recently in our church an Internal Revenue agent stood up to give a testimony and described how a great change had come into his life. He told how going through the tax returns he came across a case in which a man who had an income of less than $5,000 a year, listed a contribution to his church of $684. So the agent decided to call on him. He went to the young man's humble cottage and knocked on the door. The man came to the door and the agent told him he was from the income tax service and he had come to talk to him about his return. He said he expected the man to squirm and tremble. Instead, the man welcomed the agent and invited him in. The agent then questioned the man about his salary of less than $5,000 and the contribution of $684 to his church. There was no flustering nor hesitant excuse; he just looked the agent in the eye and said that it was his tithe and a small offering that he gave to his Lord. The agent asked for receipts as proof and the young man was able to produce them for he kept them in the drawer where he kept his church envelopes. The agent said everything was correct, apologized, and was about to leave when the man invited him to attend his church. The agent thanked him and told him he belonged to a church already. Then the young man said, "Excuse me, sir, but somehow that possibility had not occurred to me."

As he drove away, the agent said the last sentence of that young man stayed in his mind: "Excuse me, sir, but somehow that possibility had not occurred to me." What did he mean? He said he never understood it until the following Sunday morning when the offering plate passed before him and he dropped in his usual quarter. He couldn't help but think of that young man. He worked with his hands — he was a day laborer — and he made less than $5,000 a year. But he had dedicated to God a tenth and had added a love offering beside.

Now I have no idea who that young man is, but in his life there is strength and he will do good. God will bless him and prosper him. Some day he may own the company he works for, for the man had been taught of the Lord and he had read from the Word of God the Lord's will for his life. Any man who does God's will is a man of strength, character, and blessedness.

THE WORD AND OUR FUTURE

All we know of the future is written in the Book. We know nothing besides and nothing else. What of the morrow? What of the grave? What of a life to come? We could go to a philosopher and ask him about tomorrow, the future. The three greatest philosophers who ever lived were Socrates, Plato, and Aristotle. Socrates' hero was Plato, and Plato in his essays writes about Socrates, and in their writings we find the highest intellectual achievement of the human mind. We ask Socrates about death and he replies that he does not know.

I ask the scientist, the man who with his instruments studies and writes his observations in volumes of books. In fact, we are told that fifty million pages of scientific discovery are published every year. I ask the scientist about life to come and the future. He writes and says it is beyond his purview of scientific discovery. Pascal, the great French scientist, said the silence of the universe terrified him. Mr. Scientist, what of the morrow? He does not know.

We are living in the day of the occult. It is sweeping America like a storm. So I go to the occult. I ask the magician about the morrow. What of the grave? What of future life? Houdini was probably the greatest magician America ever knew, and he was followed by one almost as great, Blackstone. Before Houdini died he made a covenant with Blackstone that his ashes were to be scattered from a bridge in Chicago, and once a year after that Blackstone, with Houdini's widow, would stand on that bridge, hold an object in his hand, and Houdini was to knock it out. Year after year Blackstone stood there with an object in his hand crying, "Houdini, where are you? Houdini, come and knock this object out my hand. Let us know that you live, that you see, that you know. Houdini." They finally quit. The magician doesn't know.

I take my question to the secularist, the man of the world. These are the men who run the military, business, and political life. I ask them about the future. What of the grave and the life to come? I remember a conversation between a young sailor and his commanding officer on one of the great battleships of the U.S. Navy as they were steaming into combat. The young fellow was afraid, and trembling he went to the officer and said, "Sir, I am afraid. Do you have a word for me about death and about the world to come?" The commanding officer replied to the sailor's question and said, "Young man, I have always felt that there was nothing but here and now, so I try to get as much pleasure out of life as I can. I know nothing of the life beyond the grave." This is the word of the whole world. The philosopher, the scientist, the magician, the man of the secular world — they do not know.

Does God have an answer? Does God speak to us? Does the Lord say words to us about the grave, about death, and about the life that is to come? Yes, on page after page after page. "Let not your heart be troubled: ye believe in God, believe also in me." Blessed Jesus, we shall. "In my Father's house are many mansions: if it were not so, I would have told you. I go to prepare a place for you. And if I go and prepare a place for you, I will come again, and receive you unto myself; that where I am, there ye may be also." Where is heaven? Where Jesus is. Where do our loved ones go? Where Jesus is. He brought life and immortality to light. Sin and darkness and disease and disaster and violence and death will not rule in this world forever. There is coming a time when God will intervene in human history. There will be a new heaven and a new earth, and we will have a new body and a new fellowship and a new city. There will be no more death nor sorrow nor crying, for these things will all pass away and under God all things will be made new. How do we know these things? They are revealed to us in the sacred Book and we can know of them in no other way. This is the Word by which the gospel is preached to you. Oh, blessed hope, precious Savior, glorious Lord!

CHAPTER 8

THE SPIRITUAL TEMPLE

1 Peter 2:1-7

Have you ever considered yourself a spiritual temple? Peter refers to this in 1 Peter 2:1-7: "Wherefore laying aside all malice, and all guile, and hypocrisies, and envies, and all evil speakings, as newborn babes, desire the sincere milk of the word, that ye may grow thereby: if so be ye have tasted that the Lord is gracious. To whom coming, as unto a living stone, disallowed indeed of men, but chosen of God, and precious, ye also, as lively stones, are built up a spiritual house, an holy priesthood, to offer up spiritual sacrifices, acceptable to God by Jesus Christ. Wherefore also it is contained in the scripture, Behold, I lay in Sion a chief corner stone, elect, precious: and he that believeth on him shall not be confounded. Unto you therefore which believe he is precious."

Peter begins by speaking of malice, guile, hypocrisy, envy, and evil speakings. He ends our passage by talking about a holy, heavenly, spiritual temple of the Lord. The contrast is impressive. Peter begins in darkness, but ends in the light — the glorious light of the redemptive goodness of God. He begins with the people estranged and ends with the holy community of the Lord. He begins with unpolished stone and ends with the perfect temple of God. He begins with the scattered units and ends with the perfect union. Do you notice also that our Lord Christ is central and foundational in the passage written by the apostle? "To whom coming, as unto a lively stone . . . chosen of God, and precious," and we are built up to God by Christ. "Unto you therefore which believe he is precious." Throughout the passage there is a lifting up of our Lord. For example, can you find a better definition of the Christian faith than this: "to whom coming"? The Christian religion is a continuous coming to the Lord. We are coming for forgiveness. We are coming for salvation. We are coming for wisdom, for direction, for blessing, for help, for encouragement, for healing.

COMING TO THE LORD

Christ illustrates this in two ways: first, as a little child who comes to father or mother, and comes again and again and again. So we come to Jesus, not one time or one day, but throughout the pilgrimage of our life. Christ illustrates it also by using the figure of a building. We are living stones, that is, we are quickened in Him. We live in Him and are built up a spiritual house. It is Christ all the way. Christianity is Christ. Jesus is the beginning, the middle, and the end. He is the same yesterday, today, and forever.

You may have traveled abroad, and you found that from place to place your guide changed. You had one guide in Rome, another in Athens, another in Israel, and an another in Moscow. It is not like that in the Christian pilgrimage. We have one guide and one leader from the beginning to the end. In the story of the children of Israel Moses led them into the wilderness, but it was Joshua who led them into the Promised Land. Not so with us. We have one leader who will lead us to our Promised Land. We have our Lord in the springtime of life, in the days of strength and energy. Our Lord is with us also in the noonday of life, bearing the burden in the heat of the day. And we also have our Lord at the eventide of life, when the way grows weary. Our Lord is with us in affluence that He might crown it. He is ours in poverty that He might console us and cheer us. He stays at our side in dishonor and shame that He might somehow lead us and help us. He is our Lord in fame and honor that He might sanctify us. He encourages us in sickness that He might heal us. He is our Lord always. That is why when a man preaches Jesus he preaches the gospel. When a missionary stands in a darkened land and lifts up the cross that is the light of the world.

Now let us notice who comes: "chosen of God, and precious." As living stones we are built up a spiritual, holy priesthood, and we offer up spiritual sacrifices to God. Jesus is the foundation upon which the spiritual house is built. He is the Holy One of Israel for whom we are high priests, and He is the great sacrifice by whom we offer up spiritual sacrifices to God.

THE SPIRITUAL HOUSE

First of all let us discuss the spiritual house, the spiritual temple of the Lord. We are a building of God's own hands, a tent He has set. When we read in the Bible about the tabernacle and the temple we notice that these were made by man's hands. But Jesus is not speaking of man-made temples; rather He is speaking of eternities that are not seen, spiritual realities. The apostle Paul said it like this: "while we look not at the things which are seen, but at the things which are not seen: for the things which are seen are temporal; but the things which are not seen are eternal" (2 Cor. 4:18). Material things are transient and pass away. That is one of the reasons why the world for centuries has looked upon Plato as one of the greatest philosophers of all time. The heart of his philosophy is that the eternities, the things that abide forever, are things of the mind. They are the ideas. For example, we say that a chair is real. Plato would say it is not so, for a chair is temporal. It will decay, burn up, or become useless. Plato says that eternity is the idea. Through the years the idea is always there. Plato taught in his philosophy the great spiritual facts God reveals in His Word. The tabernacle, the temple, the house of brick or gold — these are temporalities. They are transient and pass away. But the eternities are the spiritual truths God would have us know.

THE TEMPLE OF GOD

So it is with the temple of God. How can you build a temple in which you could contain omnipresence? How can you put God under a roof? The Lord is teaching us a couple of truths. First, the temple of God is you. God dwells in you as a temple. One time the Lord told the Jewish nation to destroy "this temple" and in three days He would build it up again. They could not understand, for it had taken six years to build the temple. And Jesus would raise it up in three days? Then John the apostle wrote: "but he spake of the temple of his body." "In the beginning was the Word . . . and the Word was made flesh . . . and we beheld his glory, the glory as of the only begotten of the Father." The word was made flesh and "tabernacled" among us. The Greek word translated by "dwelt" actually means God dwells in the mind and soul of an intelligent and spiritually regenerated man. That is why the apostle Paul said, "Know ye not that your body is the temple of the Holy Ghost? . . . ye are not your own? For ye are bought with a price: therefore, glorify God in your body" (1 Cor. 6:19,20). The temple of the Lord is you.

Also, the temple of the Lord is the household of faith. Living stones are built up into a spiritual house. Empty a church building and it is dead. But we are living stones built up into a living house. The temple of God is the convocation of His people and He lives among us. We are built up into a living house of the Lord; and, as such, He gathers us together. We are separated from the mass and are

quickened and made a part of the household of faith. When we are all
together, there are we the heavenly, perfect temple of our blessed
Jesus.

A HOLY PRIESTHOOD

Second, coming unto God we are built up a holy priesthood. That
means you. In the ancient tabernacle and temple we would see a
priest dressed in beautiful robes ministering before an earthly shrine.
But Peter is not talking about such a priest. We are priests, chosen of
God, born into the priesthood by regeneration. In the first chapter of
the Book of Revelation John writes about Him who "loved us, and
washed us from our sins in his own blood, and hath made us kings and
priests unto God and his Father; to him be glory and dominion for
ever and ever." Just think of that. We are priests by birth. The priest
in the Old Testament had to be born a son of Aaron. He was born into
the priesthood, and we also are born into it. When you were born
again, regenerated, you were born into the high priestly office. When
the Old Testament priest was consecrated for his task, the blood of
the sacrificial victim was placed on the lobe of his ear, on the thumb of
his hand, and on the big toe of his foot. He was consecrated by the
blood. That is, he was to hear the word of God so the blood was
touched to his ear. He was to do the work of God, so blood was placed
on his hand. And he was to walk in the way of the Lord, so the blood
was placed on his foot. We are high priests consecrated to listen, to
do, and to walk. The priest represented God to man and man to God.
We also are to do that — witnessing, testifying, pointing others to the
blessed Jesus. We probably can find many people who would say he
or she was pointed to Christ by a friend, a mother, a father, a saintly
pastor.

Not only are we built up into the temple of the Lord, and not only
are we chosen to be high priests ministering before God, but we are
chosen also to offer up spiritual sacrifices acceptable to the Lord.
What kind of sacrifice is a spiritual sacrifice? It is an offering to the
Lord and is given wholly to Him.

A CONTRITE HEART

When we turn to the Word of God we see a number of spiritual
sacrifices offered to God. In Psalm 51 David says, "For thou desirest
not sacrifice; else would I give it: thou delightest not in burnt offering.
The sacrifices of God are a broken spirit: a broken and a contrite
heart, O God, thou wilt not despise." So a spiritual sacrifice is a
broken spirit and a contrite heart. Lord, forgive me if I am proud.
Forgive me if I am selfish and try to place myself first. Forgive me if I

am self-seeking. Forgive me if I am rebellious. Forgive me if I am not submissive and yielded. Lord, I am nothing but dust and ashes. You are so mighty and so great. I am what I am by the grace of God. It is a beautiful thing to offer to God the sacrifices of a contrite spirit.

A Loving Heart

There is also the sacrifice of a loving heart. One day a scribe came to the Lord and asked Him what was the greatest commandment of all. Jesus answered him by saying: "Thou shalt love the Lord thy God with all thy heart, and with all thy soul, and with all thy mind. This is the first and great commandment. And the second is like unto it, Thou shalt love thy neighbour as thyself." What could be greater than that a man love God with all his heart, his soul, and his mind, and his neighbor as himself? That is more than all the burnt offerings we could imagine. Rather than burnt offerings and sacrifices, we are to love God and to love His people.

A Living Sacrifice

Another spiritual sacrifice is spoken of in Romans 12. "I beseech you, therefore brethren, by the mercies of God, that ye present your bodies a living sacrifice, holy, acceptable unto God, which is your reasonable service." What are the spiritual sacrifices we offer God? The house in which I live, the tabernacle in which God has given me to dwell. That is why it is sad to see a young person take the body given by God and fill it with drugs and wrong it. When we see young people defame the body, the house of God, we can't help but hurt on the inside. The things that follow in a life and a circle like that are devastating. God asks us to dedicate our bodies as a dwelling place for the Spirit of the Lord.

And then let us listen to a beautiful word from Hebrews 13: "By him therefore let us offer the sacrifice of praise to God continually, that is, the fruit of our lips giving thanks in his name. But to do good and to communicate forget not: for with such sacrifices God is well pleased." What are the sacrifices we offer to God? The praise of our lips — just thanking God for every step of the way. The Lord has been so good to us. We feel like traveling on until we can see those mansions above, just blessing God for every step of the way. What a sweet and blessed way. "This is the way, walk ye in it."

CHAPTER 9

THE SIN-BEARER

1 Peter 2:19-24

Among the many titles given to our Lord, that of "sin-bearer" is one filled with meaning. "For this is thankworthy [*charis* — grace], if a man for conscience toward God endure grief, suffering wrongfully. . . . For even hereunto were ye called: because Christ also suffered for us, leaving us an example, that ye should follow his steps: who did no sin, neither was guile found in his mouth: who, when he was reviled, reviled not again; when he suffered, he threatened not; but committed himself to him that judgeth righteously: who his own self bare our sins in his own body on the tree, that we, being dead to sins, should live unto righteousness." Our text picks up a theme the apostle began in his first chapter. He is writing to the *diaspora,* the Christian Jews. Because of the persecution that arose after Nero blamed the Christians for the burning of Rome, the provinces were undergoing a great trial. The apostle writes in the first chapter that though they were now in heaviness through these trials, they were to remember that the trial of their faith was more precious than gold. He repeats the thought in the beginning of our text in verse 19. "For this is *charis* — grace, if a man for conscience toward God endure grief, suffering wrongfully."

OUR LORD'S FLOCK

We see in our text our Lord's attitude toward His flock. It is as if the Savior had said to the world, "These are My sheep; this is My flock. Take them and torment them." And the world did just that. From the beginning the little flock of our Lord was afflicted and tormented. They were broken on the rack, they were burned at the stake, they were drowned in water, and until Constantine and his government outlawed crucifixion, they were nailed to the tree. They were fed to the wild beasts. In the great coliseums tier upon tier of bloodthirsty spectators looked down into the arena, shouting and cheering as the Christians were delivered to the lions. As the iron cages were opened, the starved and ferocious beasts were turned loose on God's flock. How did the Christians react? Did they deny His name? Did they recant the faith?

We get a glimpse of the persecutions in *Fox's Book of Martyrs*, one of the greatest volumes ever penned. The purpose of that book is to show us how God's little flock did under terrible persecution. One young Christian named Blandinia received such strength when she was tortured that it amazed her persecutors. Marcus, Bishop of Arethusa, was smeared with honey, and angered wasps stung him to death. A little band of Christians was covered with pitch and set on fire, and with their flaming, burning hands, clapping in the presence of the Lord, they repeated, "None but Jesus — Jesus only." It almost seems as though it pleased God to feed His little flock to the blood-thirsty world. There has never been an age nor a generation since that time which has known such tragic suffering on the part of the Christian. The Lord only knows what has happened to God's children in North Korea, in Communist China, and in mad Uganda. All of this is going on at the present time. God's little flock has always suffered grief unjustly. And the inspired apostle tells us that this is our calling. Christ suffered for us, leaving us an example. Our Lord, in whom was found no sin, neither guile in His mouth, when He was reviled did not revile again. When He suffered, He did not threaten but committed Himself to God.

Peter writes out of a personal experience. He was present when the Lord was betrayed. When our Lord was arrested, Peter was there at the trial before the members of the Sanhedrin, and finally before Pontius Pilate. He saw Jesus crucified — saw Him bow His head in agony and die. Peter watched all that, and he also observed the quiet bearing of our Lord. He saw the taunts, the mockery, the scourging and suffering, and finally the crucifixion of the Son of God. I can well believe that those tragic hours of the passion and death of our Lord made an impact on Peter's mind and brought tears to his eyes. He is our example, says Peter, and we are called to follow.

We must not think that the death of our Lord was only exemplary. Lest we think Christ's death was just an example for us, the apostle continues, "who his own self bare our sins in his own body on the tree." His death was far more than an example; it was also expiatory. It was a propitiation, it was for the purpose of bearing our sins away. Had the death of our Lord been just an example, it would have been nothing more than that of a great hero, but the death of Christ was in behalf of us who are sinners, so that someday we can see God's face and live.

SIN AND PUNISHMENT

As I approach that awesome sight of Christ on the cross I should take off my shoes, for the ground on which I stand is holy. I feel that I ought to kneel and bow my head in confession as I think of that moment of all time and history. "Who his own self bare our sins in his own body on the tree."

Every sin carries with it a punishment. No man can break that iron chain. God created the universe like that. Sin and judgment go together — the soul that sins shall surely die. The wages of sin is death. But the punishment that should come upon us He took upon Himself. The cup that we could not drink, He drank. The suffering we could not bear, He bore in our stead. There is more. Not only did He bear the judgment and the penalty that should fall upon us for our sins, but He also took upon Himself our sins in His own self — in His own body on the tree.

It is impossible for me to explain that to you for I do not understand it all. I just know God's Word says that He did it. God transferred to Himself all the sin we have ever committed or ever will commit. How could God do that? I do not know. It is an inexplicable mystery. It is something God has not chosen to reveal to us, but God actually took our sins and placed them upon the Lord Jesus. Somehow He is the second Adam. He is the representative man and as such all the sins of the world are placed on Him. As in the first man, Adam, all of us were cursed and died, so in the second Adam all of us are blessed and made alive. He is the shepherd of our souls. All we as sheep have gone astray, but we are now returned unto the shepherd and bishop of our souls. He is the great representative keeper, and somehow God has made Him chargeable for each member of the flock. He is held accountable for all the wrongdoing in our lives — all of it is placed on His account. I do not understand that. I just say it. I am just an echo of what God's Book reveals to us. Had Christ died a hero, had He given His life for some great altruistic cause, the Father in heaven could have looked down on Him and said, "This is My Son. I am so proud of Him. I congratulate Him. Look, He is giving His life for the people." That could have happened, but it did not. What actually happened was that when the Lord went to the cross bearing the sins of the world, God made Him to be sin for us. Instead of God looking down in commendation and congratulations, the Gospels say that the Lord turned His face away. God hid His face and the Son died crying, "My

God, my God, why hast thou forsaken me?" In a mystery that lies in the heart of God He became our sin.

The apostle uses an unusual word for "bare" — *anaphero*. It is a word you would use in describing a man who is bearing a sacrifice up before God. He is taking an offering up before God to slay it. In it also is the idea of stooping under a great weight, like an Atlas with the weight of the world on his shoulders. Our Lord stooped and on Him was placed the burden of all the sins of all humanity, and He bore it to the cross and there made atonement for our sins. The apostle, by inspiration, points to the One who is doing it. Is that not a wonderful thing?

Are we saved by a dogma? No. Are we saved by a doctrine? No. Are we saved by a system of theology? No. We are saved by a Someone. Who can forgive sins but God? When the Lord told the paralytic his sins were forgiven, the Pharisees were correct when they murmured saying, "This man blasphemed." Who can forgive sins but God? Where they were incorrect was that Jesus was more than a man. Jesus is the God-man, and the God-man can forgive sin. A man brought death into the world and a man must take it away. The God-man was able to do for us what we could not do for ourselves — bear in Himself our redemption and salvation. He had to be divinely strong, yet humanly compassionate. Somehow he had to be forever preexistent and at the same time capable of dying. He had to be one who kept the law and yet who died as though He were transgressor of it. We see grace on grace. Where sin abounded, there grace abounded much more. And we see Him as the only begotten of the Father, full of grace and truth, for the law came by Moses but grace came by Jesus Christ. However the mountain of sin may rise in this world, the mountain of God's loving grace in Christ is abounding more and more. Passover night there was a lamb to substitute for the families but there is no substitute for Christ. When the high priest came on the day of atonement and slew a lamb and offered it before God, the sacrifice was in behalf of the nation, but when Christ was offered for the sins of the world there was no sacrifice for Him. He took it upon Himself. The whole life of our Lord was vicarious.

Our Lord's Compassion

In Matthew 8 we read of the Lord healing people from early morn until evening. Matthew writes "that it might be fulfilled which was spoken by Esaias the prophet, saying, Himself took our infirmities, and bare our sicknesses." I think the Lord suffers for every one of us, and when we are grieved I think He is grieved. When we are sick I think He is hurt and I think He is moved by our weaknesses. We see this illustrated often in His life. On the cross He was bearing our weaknesses and our sins.

MADE ALIVE TO RIGHTEOUSNESS

Our text also speaks of a quickening. We who were dead to sins are made alive to righteousness. That is as miraculous an act as anything we can find under the hand of God. We see the effect the preaching of the gospel has upon a human heart when that heart opens and invites the Lord in. Once we were dead to sin but now are alive to God. Sin loses its allurement, its attractiveness. We become dead to it and we see its real character when we accept Christ. False prophets come with veils over their faces, supposedly to hide their glory. But something always happens to show us these people as they really are.

When we were in London the Maharajah Guru held a convocation of all his followers, and they marched through the streets of London by the thousands. I stood there and just watched them march by. Recently he was in Houston at the Astrodome, and many of his followers bowed down and kissed his feet and worshiped him as the great messiah. If you are a Christian you cannot bow down and kiss his feet and accept him as the true messiah. There is something inside of you that rebels. To you it is offensive and repulsive. You know the Lord and something has happened to you. You are a different kind of person; you are dead to sin and alive to God. That is the most remarkable thing that happens to a man when he is saved. His language is different. His interests are different. He is alive to that to which others are dead. He is dead to that to which others are alive. The man who opens his heart to faith in Christ has a new love, a new vision, a new hope, a new life, a new dream, a new way, a new goal, a new tomorrow. He has been saved.

CHAPTER 10

THE FACE OF SEVERITY

1 Peter 3:10-12

It is not easy or enjoyable to speak of the wrath or severity of God, but it is something we need to hear. Peter writes on this theme in 1 Peter 3:10-12: "For he that will love life, and see good days, let him refrain his tongue from evil, and his lips that they speak no guile: let him eschew evil and do good; let him seek peace, and ensue it. For the eyes of the Lord are over the righteous, and his ears are open unto their prayers: but the face of the Lord is against them that do evil." I would like to dwell on this phrase, "but the face of the Lord is against them that do evil."

Some years ago I wrote a book entitled *Did Man Just Happen?* In it I described the difference between a man and a beast. One difference is that a man has a countenance. The light of knowledge and of spiritual intuition and sensitivity is in his face. He is made in the image of God and the image of the Lord is reflected in his face. Our text tells us that the countenance of the Lord is intensely moved against that which is evil. Peter describes the Lord's face as one of severity as it moves against that which is evil and against those who do evil.

THE PREACHING OF PUNISHMENT

F. B. Meyer was a famous British preacher who lived in the last century. He was a compatriot of Alexander Maclaren and Charles Haddon Spurgeon. Meyer in one of his writings mentions a convocation he attended in which there were about four hundred missionaries. As the missionaries told their stories of how they were saved, Meyer said he was astonished, as were the others, that almost all referred to the fact that when they were saved, they were moved by some message that concerned the judgment and the terror of the Lord. I remember this because that was true of my experience as a boy. The message of the judgment of God, of hell and damnation, moved me to terror as a boy and brought conviction to my soul. I do not understand the modern theological approach to God and to the preaching of His Word. It seems that there are fads in theology and fads in preaching such as we find fads in clothing and fads in cultural thinking and life. You would think that theology would be a great revelation of God presented faithfully; therefore, as God does not change, the theological message would not change. But that is not true. In the days of Jonathan Edwards divines preached on the judgment of God, and upon hell and damnation. One of the most famous sermons ever delivered by Edwards was entitled "Sinners in the Hands of an Angry God." Edwards read his sermons and did not have a powerful delivery; yet when the people heard this sermon they cried out in terror as though they were over the very pit and flames of hell itself. In this age you seldom hear hell mentioned. There are children and children's children who have attended churches in our modern America who have never heard a message on hell or damnation or the judgment of almighty God.

What is our text telling us when it speaks of severity, the face of the Lord against those who do evil? First, let me say that it is because of the goodness of God that He reveals this truth to us. It is either true or it is not true. If it is true then how gracious it is of God to reveal it to us like a railroad crossing with a warning light or a red light blinking. Or it is like a bottle labeled with a skull and crossbones signifying poison.

ILLUSTRATIONS OF GOD'S PUNISHMENT

Peter writes that the face of the Lord is against those who do evil. We see this illustrated in the entire Bible. In Genesis 3 we read of the sweet fellowship between the Lord and the man and woman He made. He created them to love Him and to be friends with Him. Mountains and oceans could not speak to the Lord and the starry universe could not think God's thoughts, so God made someone who could talk to Him and respond to Him. Therefore He made the man and his wife in His image. In the cool of the day He would visit and talk with them. One day while the Lord was away, the man and his wife disobeyed the mandate of God. When the Lord came to visit His friends He could not find them. He lifted up His voice and called, "Where are you, Adam?" and Adam replied, "I'm hiding. My wife and I are naked and we are ashamed in Your presence." And the Lord asked, "Who told you you were naked? And why are you afraid?" After Adam told God of his sin, the Lord cursed the ground Adam had to work. Look at it today. We see God's face of severity in the great deserts, howling hurricanes, thistles, briars, and weeds. The Lord God cursed also the woman and the man, and He drove them out into death. The God presented to you as a sweet, motherly soul who is indifferent to the sin and rebellion of mankind is not the God we know in history or in the revelation of the Bible.

As we turn to Genesis 6 we see the earth filled with violence and murder. The Lord God said His spirit would not always strive with man. For one hundred twenty years Noah, preacher of righteousness, pled with his generation without a convert. At the end of that time God said it was enough. He took Noah and his family, put them in an ark, shut the door, and broke up the heavens so that it rained for forty days and forty nights. Outside of those in the ark, not one soul survived the flood.

We could read page after page of Scripture and find examples such as these illustrated often. God is a God of severity and His face is set against sin. The New Testament also gives us many illustrations. In one we see Christ chasing the moneychangers out of the temple and in another He denounces the scribes and Pharisees. Just take your Bible and read of the many instances in which Christ turned against evil.

It is interesting to note that sources other than the Bible speak of the severity of God. In our twentieth century, possibly the greatest historian was Arnold Toynbee, the famous British educator and writer. *Time* magazine, in reviewing Toynbee's study of history, said, "Toynbee shattered the frozen pattern of historical determinism and materialism by openly avowing that God is a moral force in history." Secularists describe what happens in time as being just something people are doing, but Toynbee said the great moral imponderable in the life of a nation lies in God. Toynbee said there have been twenty-one civilizations in the history of mankind. Sixteen of them have already perished and Toynbee feels that without exception all sixteen perished because they were inwardly decadent. They fell because of unrighteousness. And I have to say here that America cannot continue as it is. It cannot live in debauchery and drunkenness and moral decay. The great imponderable that lies in the history of a nation lies in the moral judgment of almighty God. What we read in the Bible is nothing other than what we see in daily experience, in human life, and in human history. Thus, if God judges us, it is, as the author of Hebrews says, a terrible thing to fall into the hands of the living God, for our God is a consuming fire. If God judges iniquity every man must stand before Him guilty.

HOPE FOR THE SINNER

Since that is true, can we ever be saved? Can a man ever look upon God's face and live? How can we ever escape the fires of hell and damnation? How can we ever be with the Lord in glory? How? That is the Good News of the gospel. How can a man who is a sinner live before the face and in the presence of God? This is the gospel. In our last chapter we discussed the fact that our blessed Lord in His own self bore our sins in His own body on the tree. By His stripes we are healed. Therefore a sinner can stand in the presence of God and live because the Lord Himself took our sins and bore our iniquities. That is the Good News. That is the gospel.

I grew up in a little town in far northwest Texas, and we attended church in a little white crackerbox of a building. My family was in church every time the door was opened and I would sit on the front seat and listen to the pastor as he preached. Some of the stories those old-time preachers used to illustrate the gospel truth often did more for me in understanding the message of Christ than the tomes of theology I have poured over in years since. How those preachers would illustrate the truth of the gospel message of Christ. One of them left a special impression on my mind. The pastor was illustrating how God took our sins and our iniquities and bore them Himself that we might be saved. A little boy in a certain family had been disobedient. The father and mother reproved him but he continued to disobey. One evening, when the little lad refused to obey father and mother, he was told he would have to be punished. He was sent to the attic where he would have to spend the night. He would have to stay there until he learned how to obey, even if it took days. So the little fellow went up to the attic to spend the night and to live on bread and water. That night the father began to turn and to toss in his bed. He finally turned toward his wife and told her he couldn't forget that little boy up there in the attic. He knew he was afraid of the dark, and he could not rest. So he took some bedding and went up to the attic. The little boy watched as his daddy made a bed by his side. "Daddy, what are you doing?" And the father replied, "Son, you have been disobedient, and I cannot rescind the punishment, but I have decided to bear it with you. I am going to stay with you." So the father stayed with the little boy all that night — the next day — and all the next night. When the two came down the stairway together it was justice and love. And the little boy never forgot.

Now I know this story is not perfect when we compare it to what God has done for us, but the spirit of that love is there. The Lord cannot be just and rescind the punishment. He cannot be holy and righteous and let us go without correction. The Lord has come down from heaven to take our punishment, and He understands all about us. If you need a friend to talk to, talk to Jesus. He is with you. If you need someone to encourage you, go to Jesus. He will see you through. If you need help in time of trouble go to Him, for He was tried in every point such as we are, though He never failed. That is the gospel. That is the Good News. At the heart of the universe is inescapable punishment for sin, but the heart of the gospel is that where sin abounded, grace abounded much more. God, moved with pity and love, became not only our creator God, but also our Redeemer and Savior. How can anyone fail to love a Lord like that?

CHAPTER 11

A REASON FOR HOPE

1 Peter 3:15

Our text for this chapter is 1 Peter 3:15: "Sanctify the Lord God in your hearts: and be ready always to give an answer to every man that asketh you a reason of the hope that is in you with meekness and fear." Peter tells the Christian to be ready always to give an answer, an *apologia*. We have taken the Greek word, *apologia*, into our language as the word apology. For years the word has had the meaning of a defense, but in recent times apology has come to refer to an asking for pardon when someone thinks he has made a mistake or has done something wrong. However, that is an added meaning to the word. The word originally meant what is in our text — an *apologia* — a defense.

Many scholars of the past have written "apologies" or a defense of their style of life. One of the most beautifully written in the English tongue is the *Apologia Pro Vita Sua* by John Henry Newman. In the first Christian centuries, when faith was so sorely tested in the Roman empire, men like Tertullian, Justin Martyr, and Athenagoras wrote in defense of the faith. And they were called the great apologists. That is the way the word is correctly used here. Peter says we are to be ready always to give an *apologia*, a defense, an answer to every man who asks us a reason for the hope that is ours. Peter does not use the word *pistis*, faith, but *elpis*, hope. The word used here is the same that is used in Acts 28 and Colossians 1. Hope in our text refers to the faith of the Christian. Peter uses the word because wherever and whenever our Christian faith comes under great trial and persecution, our creed takes on a color for the future. Christians who are under great trial and persecution have a tendency to lift up their hearts and their faces to a redemption the Lord will bring when He comes again. Thus hope as expressed in Peter's epistle refers to the faith of the child of Christ. Therefore Peter admonishes the believer to be ready always to give an answer to anyone who asks why he has a hope within him. Let us look at some of the reasons.

OUR FAITH

First of all, it is because of our faith. Some people look upon religion as a crutch. They feel they are self-sufficient and are able to stand on their own feet. It might be all right for weak women and unknowledgeable children, but they do not need it. Let us consider this kind of thinking for a moment. So a man is self-sufficient. He stands on his own feet. He does not need God and he does not need Christ as Savior. In 1912 the *Titanic* made its maiden voyage from Liverpool, where it was built, to New York City. On that famous "unsinkable ship," there were 1600 of the socially elite of both continents — America and Europe. But that night in the North Atlantic the *Titanic* brushed a great iceberg and tore away a part of its right side. The ship began slowly to sink, and as it went down the dance orchestra, which had been playing for the happy guests that night, withdrew to the bow of the ship. There they began to play again and this time it was "Nearer My God to Thee." As the 1600, including that orchestra, sank into the waters, they heard the strains of that Christian hymn. The unbeliever still says it is a crutch and he does not need it. Is he sure?

Something similar happened in 1915 when the *Lusitania* was sunk by a German U-boat. This was the act which precipitated the entrance of America into the First World War. When the *Lusitania* went down, a group of singers aboard, called The Royal Welch Male Choir, in their desperation were clinging to a disabled life raft. As the life raft began to disintegrate, the men began to sing. Do you know what they sang? Let me tell you.

> Abide with me: fast falls the eventide;
> The darkness deepens; Lord, with me abide:
> When other helpers fail, and comforts flee,
> Help of the helpless, O abide with me!

But it is a crutch. Are you sure? I believe there comes a time in every person's life when he desperately needs God, but he has to know where to find Him.

FELLOWSHIP IN THE CHURCH

Be ready always to give an answer to anyone who asks you a reason for the hope that is in you. When a person responds to the Lord he is received into the fellowship of the church by baptism. When a man belongs to Christ God puts him in Christ. When a man belongs to the church, God puts him in it. You see, the church will be the church triumphant someday. God's redeemed will be gathered before His throne of glory someday, and to that church a man is joined by the baptism of the Holy Spirit. I also belong to the church visible, which we call the church militant. The church is in a constant battle against the forces of evil. Thus when a man accepts Christ and receives Him in his heart, he becomes a member of the church triumphant. To become a member of the visible church he must be baptized and make a public announcement of his faith. Who receives him? The people who already belong to the Lord. When a new believer comes to the First Baptist Church of Dallas and announces that he wants to be baptized, the entire church receives him because he will be a part of them.

The Lord Is Coming

Be ready always to give an answer to anyone who asks you a reason for the hope that is in you. Remember, the Lord is coming. One out of every four verses of the New Testament refers to the coming of the Lord, and there are many verses in the Old Testament that also refer to the second coming of Christ, more than to the first coming.

Whenever a child tells me he or she wishes to be baptized and become a member of the church I ask the child what the Lord meant when He closed the Last Supper with the words, "til he come." And there has never been a child who has failed to answer: "That means Jesus is coming again." Then I will ask the youngster, "Do you believe that?" "Yes." And I will say, "Do you believe you will see Jesus some day?" And the child will always answer, "Yes, I do." I do, too. Paul calls that the blessed hope.

A number of years ago Japan overran Korea, and for many years Korea was a part of the Japanese empire. The Japanese at that time worshiped Emperor Hirohito as a god. They accepted the Shinto religion and that religion worships the Japanese emperor as god. When the Japanese overran Korea and subjugated the nation, it came to the attention of the military commanders that the Baptist missionaries and preachers were presenting another Lord — Jesus. So, the head of the Baptist Convention in Korea was brought before the commanding officer and questioned concerning Christ. The Korean pastor told the story of Christ's life and followed it through until he finally came to where He was raised from the dead and ascended to heaven. Then what? And the pastor boldly and unashamedly replied; He's coming again — He's coming back. And the commanding officer asked, Then what? Bravely the Korean pastor continued that when

He comes, every knee shall bow and every tongue confess that He is Lord to the glory of God the Father. The commanding officer asked the pastor if that included his emperor, and the pastor said, Yes. But the emperor is god — he is divine. The Baptist pastor bravely replied that when the Lord comes, even the emperor will bow his knee and confess with his tongue that there is just one Lord and one God — Jesus. The commanding officer asked if all the Baptist pastors believed that. And the president of the convention replied that all of them believed that. Therefore the Japanese military took every Baptist pastor in the nation of Korea and put him in prison, and kept him there throughout the years of that occupation. Almost all of them died in prison and the man who was president of the convention outlived the occupation by just a few months. These pastors literally laid down their lives for the hope we have in Christ Jesus and shall I ever be afraid or ashamed to preach that blessed hope?

> Must I be carried to the skies on flowery beds of ease,
> While others fought to win the prize and sailed through bloody seas?
> Are there no foes for me to face? Must I not stem the flood?
> I'll bear the toil, endure the pain, supported by Thy word.

I make no apology, I have no feeling of self-condemnation when I preach the coming again of our blessed Lord. I do not think there is any hope in the Middle East or anywhere else for that matter, save in that One whose name is called Wonderful, Counselor, the Mighty God, the Everlasting Father, the Prince of Peace. Ah, to lift Him up, to preach His name, and to invite souls to love Him and follow Him is the highest heavenly privilege of human life.

CHAPTER 12

CHRIST IN HADES

1 Peter 3:17-22

I would dare say that 1 Peter 3:18,19 is one of the most difficult of all of the passages in the Bible. Beginning at verse 17 we read: "For it is better, if the will of God be so, that ye suffer for well-doing, than for evil-doing. For Christ also hath once suffered for sins, the just for the unjust, that he might bring us to God, being put to death in the flesh, but quickened by the Spirit: by which also he went and preached unto the spirits in prison; which sometime were disobedient, when once the longsuffering of God waited in the days of Noah, while the ark was a-preparing, wherein few, that is, eight souls were saved by water. The like figure whereunto even baptism doth also now save us (not the putting away of the filth of the flesh, but the answer of a good conscience toward God,) by the resurrection of Jesus Christ: who is gone into heaven, and is on the right hand of God; angels and authorities and powers being made subject unto him."

CHRIST QUICKENED BY THE SPIRIT

In this difficult passage we see our Lord not only being put to death in the flesh, but also being quickened by the Spirit by which He also went and preached to the spirits in prison, those spirits who were disobedient in the days of Noah when the longsuffering of God waited for their repentance. What does that mean? I used to say that this passage referred to the spirit of Christ in Noah when Noah preached for 120 years, pleading with his hearers to repent. It was the spirit of Christ in the preacher who was pleading with them. I probably said that because I was afraid to admit that I did not know the real meaning of the passage and could not understand it — and still do not understand it fully. Many great scholars agree with this interpretation. But when I take another look at the text, I cannot escape the persuasion that that interpretation is not right. Let us look at our text together.

In verse 18 we read that Christ, being put to death in the flesh, was quickened by the Spirit — a capital "S." The translators of this text in the King James Version believed that the text says that Christ, being put to death in the flesh, was quickened by the Holy Spirit. There is nothing wrong with that, certainly. Paul, in Romans 1:4 declares that Christ was raised from the dead by the Holy Spirit of God. Our problem begins with the words following: "By which also he went and preached unto the spirits in prison." What does that mean?

PREACHING IN THE SPIRIT

Christ was not put to death in the flesh, but was quickened in the Spirit — *pneumati*. His spirit was quickened, and in that spirit he went and preached to the spirits in prison. He did not go to preach to the spirits in prison when He was raised from the dead, as the King James Version seems to imply. Let me go over that again. It was not when Christ was raised from the dead that in His new resurrection body He went down to Hades and preached to the spirits in prison. Our text tells us that being put to death He was quickened in the spirit, in which spirit He went down into hell to preach to the spirits in that prison. Our Lord Jesus Christ was glorious in His spiritual efforts before He became a sacrifice for our sins. Before Christ was incarnate, He was pure spirit, and He was glorious in spiritual majesty. When Christ was separated from His body — when He was put to death — His spirit was quickened.

It is an amazing thing the apostle is writing here. Peter is writing to the persecuted Jewish Christians of Asia Minor, and he is telling them to take heart and not be discouraged. It is a part of the divine family of God to suffer. Abel, Job, Jeremiah, even our Lord suffered. He was put to death, but His crucifixion, Peter is saying, did not lessen His power or the glory of His influence. Rather, it was augmented, and when the Lord suffered and died He went down where in the days of His flesh He could not have gone. As long as the Lord was in His flesh, He was separated from the ability to be conversant with the spirit world. But when He died, His sphere of influence was enlarged; and in this larger sphere He preached to those who were in Hades. So Peter told the suffering Christians not to be discouraged, for their suffering, even if it led to martyrdom, enlarged their witness and testimony for Christ.

CHRIST IN HADES

F. B. Meyer, the noble Baptist preacher of London, England, of the past century, describes in an eloquent passage the descent of the king of Babylon into another world — into hell. Using Isaiah 14:16 as a background, he describes the king as being a pale ghost, and as he comes down into another world, having finally met the fate of death from the hands of almighty God, he is greeted by the thin voices of the ghost and the shadows of the kings he has slain and the chiefs of the people he has decimated. In tones of withering sarcasm the shadows say to the king of Babylon as he descends into their midst, "What? Are you weak like us and are you come down to us? You, who made the earth to tremble and made the kingdoms of the world shake? You, coming down to us, who are pale, thin ghosts?" If Isaiah presents the stirring in another world at the coming down of the great king of Babylon, can you imagine the stirring in another world when the Son of God came down?

In Ephesians 4:8,9, Paul says: "When he ascended up on high, he led captivity captive, and gave gifts unto men. (Now that he ascended, what is it but that he also descended first into the lower parts of the earth?)" When you study these verses closely, you come to the conclusion I have come to. Paul says our Lord in His death descended into the lower parts of the earth and to a Jewish people. This means that when one descended into the lower parts of the earth, it was another world — Sheol. Paul and Peter have written what the church has proclaimed from the beginning.

Look at the Apostles' Creed. "I believe in God the Father Almighty, maker of heaven and earth; and in Jesus Christ His only Son, our Lord; who was conceived by the Holy Ghost, born of the Virgin Mary, suffered under Pontius Pilate, was crucified, dead, and buried; he descended into hell; the third day he rose again from the dead; he ascended into heaven, and sitteth at the right hand of God the Father Almighty; from thence he shall come to judge the quick and the dead. I believe in the Holy Ghost; the holy Catholic Church; the communion of saints; the forgiveness of sins; the resurrection of the body; and the life everlasting. Amen." Did you follow its historical order? "I believe in Jesus Christ, conceived by the Holy Ghost, born of the Virgin Mary, suffered under Pontius Pilate, was crucified, dead, and buried. He descended into hell. Then the third day He rose again from the dead."

(margin annotation: Apostles Creed.)

Preaching in Hades

The faith of the Christian church expressed in the Apostles' Creed is exactly the order in which the apostle Peter writes it here. Jesus was put to death in the flesh, He was quickened by the Spirit in which spirit He went and preached to the spirits in prison before He was

t take place after He was raised from

only about those who were disobe-
about all the other spirits who were
ods of the church? We may suppose
are not named, but that is not so. For
pressed by the Flood of Noah. For
of the Noahic Flood and in 3:5,6 he
ade a great impression on his mind
being especially disobedient, since
h's preaching.

ALWAYS LOST

nd unrepentance, and he is in hell,
be preached to him and that he can

s way. First, there is no suggestion
at a man has a second chance when
onfirmed. The Book of Ecclesiastes
it lie. When a man dies, he is dying
forever. If he dies in unbelief, he is
t, he dies lost forever.
asked, does a man have a second
ned in hell? There are two words
r proclaiming. The one most often
ns to announce good news, and our
But there is also another word and
ublicize, to herald. And that is all.
up and down the streets heralding
to Hades He went down to herald

confirm the damnation of the lost,
they were lost. That seems a little
We just know He did it. When we
Peter and ask him to tell us what it
tells us that secret things belong to
led belong to us and our children
hat we can preach.

OF BAPTISM

omparison. Speaking of those who
d also mentioning the salvation of

Noah and his family, Peter refers to the baptism that saves us. It is not the putting away of the flesh, but the answer of a regenerated heart to God. I believe Peter is saying that the water destroyed the old world. It was full of violence and sin, so the water buried it. Then out of the old world, in the rebirth of the Flood, there came a new world, purged of sin; and when Noah came out of the ark, he came into a new life and a new world. The waters of the Flood must have made the earth verdant, and there was no crime. The earth was new and Noah entered into that new earth and that new life. Peter says that is the figure wherein baptism brings us through the same experience. The water held up the ark and saved Noah and his family. It is a figure of our baptism in the water — we are buried and the old world is gone. We are dead to the old delights, the old tastes, the old visions and dreams, the old longings. We are buried under the flood and are born into a new life in Christ.

Then, lest someone think that baptism does it, Peter writes in parenthesis that it is not the putting away of the filth of the flesh, but the regenerating power of God that does it. He was writing to Jewish people who knew all about baptizing. They baptized their pots and pans, their feet, their hands, their heads — sometimes they baptized themselves all over. Peter says our baptizing is a symbol and a figure of a great spiritual reality that we have died to the old world, and, buried beneath the flood, we are raised to a new life in Christ. If any man is in Christ Jesus, he is a new creation; old things are passed away, and all things are become new. We experience a new life, a new hope, a new vision in Christ. Once we were lost, but now we are saved. This is the gospel of the grace of the Son of God.

CHAPTER 13

CRUCIFIED AND ASCENDED

1 Peter 3:18-22

In our last chapter we discussed the descent of Christ into hell, into Hades. Now we are going to discuss the first and last part of that passage as found in verses 18,21, and 22: "For Christ also hath once suffered for sins, the just for the unjust, that he might bring us to God. . . . by the resurrection of Jesus Christ: who is gone into heaven, and is on the right hand of God; angels and authorities and powers being made subject unto him." And let us consider especially these words: "that he might bring us to God." What a statement! It means that we were away from God — we were lost. You apply the word "lost" to any soul and it creates deep emotion. In one of his lamentations, Jeremiah, the weeping prophet, cried, "The harvest is past, the summer is ended, and we are not saved. . . . Oh that my head were waters, and mine eyes a fountain of tears, that I might weep day and night for the slain of the daughter of my people" (Jer. 8:20; 9:1). Jeremiah's cry was a desire to bring his people back to God.

CHILDREN OF GOD BY ADOPTION

The concept of being lost is a direct contradiction to the cheap, shallow, modern theology that says all are saved and all are children of God, and the assignment of the preacher is just to make a man aware that he is saved, making him cognizant of the fact that he is a child of God. Without exception the entire revelation of the Bible tells us that by nature we are not children of God but are children of wrath. There is no such thing in the Bible as the teaching of the universal fatherhood of God. It does not make sense that Christ should die so He might bring us to God, if we are already with God. What an idiocy to have the apostles and prophets write that we are like lost sheep, that we are dead in trespasses and in sin, that by

81

nature we are children of wrath, and that Christ came into the world to deliver us from our offenses and to present us in justification to God, when all the while we were already justified, and were already sons of heaven. In John 1:11,12 the apostle writes that the Lord "came unto his own, and his own received him not. But as many as received him, to them gave he power to become the sons of God, even to them that believe on his name." We become the sons of God by trusting in Christ. To be born only of the flesh is to be lost — we must be born again to become children of God.

We see this illustrated in Galatians 4 where the apostle Paul writes that God sent forth His Son into the world "that we might receive the adoption of sons." In the next verse Paul says that "God hath sent forth the Spirit of his Son into your hearts, crying, Abba, Father." Tell me, did you ever hear of a man adopting his own son? It would be ridiculous. He is already his son. The father would adopt a boy who is not his son. So it is with our relationship to God. We were not children of the Father. We were lost and in Christ we found redemption and forgiveness, and we have been adopted into the family of God. Christ suffered for our sins that He might bring us to God.

GOD AND OUR SINS

There are three ways in which God can deal with us in our sins. First, the Lord can condemn and consign us all to perdition. He can destroy us. Second, the Lord can disregard His law of righteousness. He can turn aside from His moral character, in which event He would plunge the world into chaos and would deny Himself. And third, God can deal with our sins by paying the debt of our wrongdoing Himself. He can make atonement for our sins. He can wash them away in the payment of blood — and that is what God chose to do. Christ suffered for our sins, the just in behalf of the unjust, that He might bring us to God. Oh, bless His name that God did not damn us. That is the gospel and that is our hope of heaven.

The far-famed English preacher, Charles Haddon Spurgeon, became seriously ill at the age of 58 and was taken to Menton, a city on the French Riviera. It was hoped that the soft breezes and the sunshine might bring health to the great pastor. Instead, he grew steadily worse and died. A friend of the great preacher was seated by his side as he lay dying, and said to him, "Mr. Spurgeon, what is your gospel now?" And the London preacher replied in four simple words: "Christ died for me." That is the gospel that will save us from our sins and bring us in salvation to God. Christ suffered for our sins, the just in behalf of the unjust, that He might bring us to God.

OUR LORD'S SUFFERINGS

The preachers of long ago used to speak of both our Lord's known and His unknown sufferings. The known sufferings of our Lord are placed before us in song, poetry, and sermons. They are dramatized before our eyes. But what are those unknown sufferings of our Lord? Isaiah speaks of them in his fifty-third chapter for he speaks as though he is on Mt. Calvary, even though he spoke 750 years before the great event. Isaiah, looking by faith, saw Christ atoning for our sins. He said God would see the travail of Christ's soul and be satisfied, and also that God would make His soul an offering for our sins. What does that mean? I do not know. Our minds cannot comprehend that great plan of God whereby our debt was paid and God was satisfied. It is just that our Lord is the life line from God to us who are perishing — the cross is the great dividing point between God and man, between heaven and hell, between hopelessness and salvation. Christ suffered for our sins that He might bring us to God.

How did He do that? It was completed by the resurrection of Jesus Christ from the dead. When you consider this truth it begins to impress you with what the apostle means. Our Lord was incarnate. He humbled Himself by coming down from heaven until He became a lowly man, a servant among us. Then He was exalted for us, raised for us. His falling down was for us and His rising again was for us. He wore the robes of our humility and our poverty that we might be clothed with the robes of His splendor. That is why the ordinance of baptism is so filled with gospel meaning. We were dead with Christ and buried. Then we were raised with Christ in a new, triumphant resurrection life. As the sea could not hold Jonah, so the grave could not hold our Lord.

OUR LORD'S RESURRECTION

After His resurrection, our Lord appeared on several occasions. He spent the forty days before His ascension with His disciples and there are two thoughts that come to mind about those days. First, those forty days of post-resurrection appearances of our Lord among His people demonstrate to us that the powers of darkness and of their leader, Satan, are forever destroyed. In the beginning of our Lord's ministry He was assailed and attacked by Satan forty days in the wilderness. Satan tempted Christ to undo the Incarnation. If Christ would only obey Satan once He would not have to suffer the agony of the cross. With three different temptations Satan buffeted our Lord, and finally saw to His death.

Now our Lord has been raised from the dead and we wonder why

Satan did not assail the Lord after that. Why did Satan not attack our Lord when He was in Galilee and at the breakfast on the shores along the lake? Why did he not challenge our Lord when He ascended to heaven? The answer is very plain — the power of Satan and the powers of the kingdoms of darkness were vanquished. They were destroyed. Christ is triumphant over sin and death, and Satan knows his time is short.

Also, those forty days in which our Lord appeared before His disciples are harbingers of the day when our Lord God Christ will return, and His feet will touch this earth. Immortalized, glorified, He will appear to His people, and He will walk in and out among His people in resurrection glory.

Our Lord's Ascension

Our Lord now has ascended into heaven and with what joy and exaltation the angels of heaven received Him. In the Book of Genesis we are told that when Israel (Jacob) returned home a host of angels met him, and Jacob called the name of the place Mahanaim, that is, two camps. The angels met Israel in great waves, welcoming him to the Promised Land. That must have been a picture of what happened in heaven when our Lord was welcomed back to glory by the angels of heaven. And heaven is our home. Our inheritance is not here — it is there. Our home is not in this earth, it is in heaven. The Lord has gone to prepare a place for us. We are strangers here — heaven is our home. I think that explains a phenomenon that took place when our Lord ascended to heaven. At that time would you not think there would be lamentation or weeping from the disciples? But there is not a hint of this. Instead, the disciples were filled with praise and thanksgiving. They knew our great Redeemer had passed beyond the veil, there to make atonement for our souls.

The battle is won, the war is over, and as victor He sits down at the right hand of authority and glory. Think of that for a moment. The great God of this universe is now a man. The Christ of the cross is also the Christ of the throne and the Christ over whom the women of Jerusalem wept. It is the same Lord Christ the angels rejoiced over and welcomed back to glory. The God of the universe is our Savior and friend. The silvery sun, the golden moon, and all the stars that shine were made by His omnipotent hands; and He is a friend of mine. When He will come with trumpet sound, all earth shall bow in the presence of that same Lord Christ, acknowledging Him to be King and God over all creation. Ah, that we might do it now. When Christ can bring to us forgiveness and hope and happiness and assurance and salvation, why not now? Let God see you through. Let God fight your battles. Let God stand by you in strength and in the hour of your death. Look to Him in faith, and at the judgment bar He will stand by your side.

CHAPTER 14

THE GOD OF JUDGMENT

1 Peter 4:17,18

Most people don't like to talk about or even think about the judgment of God, but it is a reality we must consider. Peter also speaks of it in 4:17,18: "For the time is come that judgment must begin at the house of God: and if it first begin at us, what shall the end be of them that obey not the gospel of God? And if the righteous scarcely be saved, where shall the ungodly and the sinner appear?" Peter rhetorically asks two questions here. First, if judgment falls on God's people, what will the end of the ungodly people be? Second, if salvation is barely secured to the righteous, what will happen to the unrepentant transgressor? It is an awesome thing to think of, so let us look at the two verses and discuss them.

Verse 1 speaks of the judgment of God upon His people. The author of Hebrews tells us that "vengeance belongeth unto me, I will recompense, saith the Lord. And again, The Lord shall judge his people. It is a fearful thing to fall into the hands of the living God. . . . For our God is a consuming fire" (Heb. 10:30,31; 12:29).

GOD JUDGES DIRECTLY

The judgment of God upon His people comes in two ways: by direct intervention with the hand of God upon us and indirectly with God allowing Satan to sift us, to afflict us.

Let us first discuss the judgment of God on us directly. We need only turn to the Old Testament from the beginning to the end, and we see many illustrations. We read of Samson, Saul, and David — the man after God's own heart. The Lord sent the prophet Nathan to him and told him the sword would never leave his house. The New Testament church also gives many examples. In Acts 5 Ananias and Sapphira lied to the Holy Spirit and, as punishment, they fell dead before the congregation in the Lord's house. Think of how many of us would still be alive if death was the punishment for lying. No wonder the next verse tells us that great fear came upon the church. Is there anyone who never has said something that was not quite the truth? In Acts 8 we see how the judgment of God fell upon Simeon who sought to buy the power of the Lord with money. We even get our word simony from this experience.

God's judgment continues as we read in Acts 12 how His judgment fell on Herod Agrippa I who died of worms. In Acts 13 we read about Elymas the sorcerer who opposed the preaching of the apostle Paul in the court of Sergius Paulus the Roman deputy and consequently was struck blind.

GOD PERMITS HIS JUDGMENT

Not only does God judge His people by direct intervention, but He also does it through His permissive will and often uses Satan. You remember the story of Job, do you not? Satan said to God, "No wonder Job serves You. You do not let the wind blow upon him. You do not let his enemies get to him. You hedge him about on every side. He does not serve You at all. Just let me have him and he will curse You to Your face." So God turned Job over into the hands of Satan. As the story progresses we get a little insight into why God at times permits us to fall into the hands of the evil one. In the Book of Job we read of his pride, but when Satan got through with him, Job said to the Lord, "I have heard of thee by the hearing of the ear: but now mine eye seeth thee. Wherefore I abhor myself, and repent in dust and ashes" (Job 42:5,6). Satan not only sifted Job; he sifted all the apostles as well. He is bold in attacking God's children. He looks upon us as a wolf looks upon a flock of sheep. To Satan all Christians fall into one of two categories: we are either hypocrites or we are deluded. Satan thinks we are stupid and that we serve God for what we can get out of it.

Satan likes to trap us. He trapped Judas by enticing him with thirty pieces of silver — and after that Judas committed suicide. Many of God's saints fall into Satan's traps. Money, ambition, advancement — all these plus many more keep people from doing the will of God.

Satan even baited Peter with fear for his life. At the encouragement of his friend, the apostle John, Peter went into the courtyard where Jesus was being tried in order to warm himself by the fire. A little maid suggested to him that he must be a disciple of Jesus because he talked like one of them. Peter cursed and said he did not know Him. When the Lord was arrested, the disciples for fear of their lives ran away.

JUDGED IN THE LIFE TO COME

Not only are the Lord's people judged in this life, but we are judged also in the life to come. The apostle Paul in 2 Corinthians 5 says that we must all stand before the judgment seat of Christ. And in 1 Corinthians he describes that judgment. He tells us that a man can have no other foundation than the Lord. If man builds on gold, silver, precious stones, wood, hay, or stubble, his work will be tried, and if his work burns, he will suffer loss, though he himself will be saved, as though he were escaping through a wall of flames. When we stand in the presence of the Almighty, think of the rubbish in our lives that is going to be burned up. How little do we actually do out of true love for Christ and for no other reason? We may sing, but it is so easy to sing in order to be heard of men. Just to sing or to preach for the glory of God, however, is another matter. How easy it is to prepare a sermon so that its language is beautiful and its logic impeccable and its delivery forceful. Then people would say what a fine message that was. But for a man to preach just to exalt our Lord or to pluck souls out of the burning — that is what God wants. When we stand at the judgment bar of God all of self and pride will be burned up, and only what is done for our blessed Lord will endure.

Now Peter says that if judgment falls upon God's people, what will be the end of those who do not obey the gospel of God? When the Lord offers mercy and pardon in His love and grace and man turns it down, what will happen to him? There is no pardon, there is no grace in rejection.

In my reading I came across one of the most unusual court decisions in American jurisprudence. It happened in the days of President Andrew Jackson and the great John Marshall was chief justice of the Supreme Court. A railway mail clerk named George Wilson, riding on the train through Pennsylvania, killed his fellow clerk. He then stole the mail and tied himself in some way with a rope. When the train arrived at its destination they found Wilson tied up, and the dead clerk lying in his own blood. Wilson told the story of how he had been assailed by bandits. His partner was killed, and he was tied up and the mail stolen. But as the officers of the law began to question Wilson, they found some discrepancies in his story. As they pounded at those facts that didn't quite fit, Wilson finally confessed that he killed his partner and had perpetrated the hoax. He was tried and sentenced to be hanged in the federal penitentiary. But as time passed, pity began to form for Wilson as so often happens. People seemed to have forgotten the dastardly act and the sorrow of the dead man's family. Because so many people began to pity Wilson, political pressure was brought upon President Jackson and he pardoned Wilson. The warden of the penitentiary told Wilson the president of the United States had pardoned him but to the astonishment of the warden and of the country the man refused to accept the pardon and said he wanted to be hanged — he wanted to die. The warden didn't know what to do so he called in the greatest legal minds and it was finally carried to the Supreme Court of the United States. The decision was handed down and was written by Chief Justice Marshall. This is what the court wrote: "A pardon is a paper, the value of which depends upon its acceptance by the person implicated. It is hardly to be supposed that one under sentence of death would refuse to accept a pardon, but if it is refused, it is no pardon. George Wilson must hang." And in the federal penitentiary at Leavenworth, Kansas, George Wilson was hanged.

The Judgment of the Lost

Let us relate this to the truth of the living God. Christ died for our sins. He was buried for our justification. He suffered that we might be forgiven. We have free and absolute pardon in Him, but if a man refuses it, it is no longer a pardon. There is nothing remaining but a fearful looking for and falling into the hands of the living God. For judgment must begin at the house of the Lord and if it begins with us, what will be the end of those who do not obey the gospel of Christ?

The second rhetorical question: If the righteous are barely saved, what will happen to the confirmed transgressor, the one who refuses the mercy and pardon of Christ? If we scarcely are able to enter in, what will happen to the man who is outside the door? Now what does Peter mean by the righteous being scarcely saved? Could it mean that the covenant of grace is loosely and barely arranged for? Was our salvation a second thought of God and is it advantageously done? Are we just barely in because God barely thought of it? No, for the Word says that our salvation was worked out by the Lamb of God who was slain before the foundation of the earth. Before God hung the worlds in space, He already planned for our salvation. Well then, does it mean that the blood of our Lord is hardly sufficient, that it is barely able to save us? No. The entire Bible presents the all-sufficiency of the atonement of our Lord. Listen to some of the verses now: "Come now, and let us reason together, saith the LORD: though your sins be as scarlet, they shall be as white as snow; though they be red like crimson, they shall be as wool" (Isa. 1:18). "And the blood of Jesus Christ his Son cleanseth us from all sin" (1 John 1:7). "And he is the propitiation for our sins: and not for ours only, but also for the sins of the whole world" (1 John 2:2). "Where sin abounded, grace did much more abound" (Rom. 5:20).

THE STRUGGLE OF THE SAVED

When Peter says the righteous may scarcely be saved does he mean that we may almost get there and then not make it? Does he mean that the Lord's children may yet apostatize? The Scriptures also answer that question. In John 10:28 our Lord says, "I give unto them eternal life; and they shall never perish." In Romans 5:10 Paul says, "If, when we were enemies, we were reconciled to God by the death of his Son, much more, being reconciled, we shall be saved by his life" — that is, the life of Christ in heaven. He is seated at the right hand of the Father to make sure that we who have trusted in Him will be finally saved. Yes, we are saved forever.

In 1 Peter 1, Peter says, "Blessed be the God and Father of our Lord Jesus Christ, which according to his abundant mercy hath begotten us again unto a lively hope by the resurrection of Jesus Christ from the dead, to an inheritance incorruptible, and undefiled, and that fadeth not away, reserved in heaven for you, who are kept by the power of God." There is no such thing as our failing at the beautiful gates. What then does it mean if the righteous scarcely be saved? Peter refers to it when he mentions the drag of the old nature that we Christians have who live in this body of flesh. Our hearts are regenerated, we have given ourselves to Jesus, we have accepted Him as our Savior; but we still live in this old house, and this old carnal nature is still a part of us and it drags us down. Every Christian knows the drag of that carnality. It is no wonder Paul cried in Romans 7:24,19: "O wretched man that I am! who shall deliver me from the body of this death? . . . For the good that I would I do not: but the evil which I would not, that I do." God's people are assailed every step of the way and we will be until this house of clay turns back to dust and God gives us a new, immortalized body.

Not only do we struggle with the drag of that old nature, but we also have the weakness of the new nature. We are born into the kingdom of heaven and we come in as little babes. A person may be sixty, seventy, or eighty years old when he is saved, but he is still a babe in Christ. I have been in the kingdom more than fifty years now, and sometimes I think of myself still as just learning the ABC's of the Christian faith. How we need help and encouragement in our Christian walk!

Not only that, but we also have the opposition of the evil one. Paul wrote to the Thessalonians that he wanted to come to them time and again, but Satan hindered him (1 Thess. 2:18). Because of Satan's opposition we are to strive — "agonize" — to enter in the straight way. Paul tells us in Galatians 5 that "the flesh lusteth against the Spirit, and the Spirit against the flesh" (Gal. 5:17). The trials and the sorrows of the Christian life can be agony.

"If the righteous scarcely be saved, where shall the ungodly and the sinner appear?" It is an awesome thing for a man to turn down the pardon of God. It is a solemnity that ought to bring a man to his knees. He needs to pray, "Lord, I need someone to forgive my sins. I need an advocate to remember me at the judgment bar of almighty God, and I need the Lord's blessings in this life, in this world, in this day and time. And, Lord, if You can mediate the mercy and the forgiveness of God to my soul, then Lord, today I take You for my Savior." Would you do that?

CHAPTER 15

FEEDING THE FLOCK

1 Peter 5:1-4

Peter's shepherd heart is revealed in the words of the text for this chapter. "The elders which are among you I exhort, who am also an elder, and a witness of the sufferings of Christ, and also a partaker of the glory that shall be revealed: Feed the flock of God which is among you, taking the oversight thereof, not by constraint, but willingly; not for filthy lucre, but of a ready mind; Neither as being lords over God's heritage, but being ensamples to the flock. And when the chief Shepherd shall appear, ye shall receive a crown of glory that fadeth not away."

The imagery of a shepherd and his flock was deep in the hearts of the people of Israel. Being a shepherd was an exalted vocation, and the reason for it is evident, for the patriarchs were shepherds. Abraham, Isaac, Jacob, the sons of Israel — all were shepherds. Moses also was a shepherd. Having fled the court of Pharaoh, he tended the flocks of Jethro, his father-in-law. He tended Jethro's sheep for forty years. David, the psalmist and sweet singer of Israel was a shepherd. So many of his psalms reflect that pastoral life, such as the Twenty-third Psalm which begins with "The LORD is my shepherd." Some of the great prophets such as Amos were shepherds. All through the Word of the Lord you will find the imagery used here by Peter. It is the same imagery we read in Acts 20 when Paul tells the Ephesian elders to "take heed therefore unto yourselves, and to all the flock over which the Holy Ghost hath made you overseers . . . feed the church of God, which he hath purchased with his own blood." The word used is *poimainō* and means "to tend, to care for." Another place where that word is used to shepherd a flock is found in John 21 where the Lord says to Peter, "Simon, do you love Me?" And Peter answers, "Lord, You know all about me. You know I love You," and the Lord said to him, *"Poimainō* — shepherd My sheep." In other words, "take care of My people."

THE SHEPHERD HEART

Let us look first at the heavenly calling of the shepherd heart. "And when the chief Shepherd shall appear, ye shall receive a crown of glory that fadeth not away." Those who take care of the flock of Christ will receive a heavenly crown. There are five crowns mentioned in the New Testament. The first is the martyr's crown: "be thou faithful unto death, and I will give thee a crown of life" (Rev. 2:10). There is also the soul winner's crown: "Will there be any stars in my crown?" Then there is the righteous crown: "I have fought a good fight, I have finished my course, I have kept the faith: henceforth there is laid up for me a crown of righteousness, which the Lord, the righteous judge, shall give me at that day: and not to me only, but unto them also that love his appearing" (2 Tim. 4:7,8). The fourth crown is the victor's crown. Paul writes in 1 Corinthians 9 of those who are engaged in athletic contests. He says they strive for a corruptible crown, but we are reaching out for an incorruptible crown.

The last crown is the pastor's crown, or the shepherd's crown. "And when the chief Shepherd shall appear, ye shall receive a crown of glory that fadeth not away." And this does not apply only to the clergy, for our text does not distinguish between the man who pastors a church and the people who belong to it. We are all one in Christ. We are all fellow servants in the ministry of the gospel of the grace of the Son of God. We may all receive the shepherd's crown.

THE SEEKING HEART

I would like to have us consider also the seeking heart. I want to address this to pastors of the flock of God. I would like to suggest that in our teaching and in our preaching there should be an appeal, a reaching out — there should always be sounded the seeking note. Listen to the Lord: "What man of you, having an hundred sheep, if he lose one of them, doth not leave the ninety and nine in the wilderness, and go after that which is lost, until he find it?" (Luke 15:4). There should always be an appeal in our churches. In 2 Timothy 4 Paul tells the young pastor of the church at Ephesus that he must do the work of an evangelist (v. 5). In Ephesians Paul wrote that "when [the Lord] ascended up on high, he led captivity captive, and gave gifts unto men" — and he names those charismatic gifts. The persons and gifts are mentioned together. He writes of apostles, prophets, evangelists, pastors, teachers. And that is the way Paul uses the word when he writes to the young pastor at the church at Ephesus. He is to do the work of an evangelist, though he is a pastor and not an evangelist. So we are to do the work of an evangelist, and our ministry is to include that seeking note — bringing people to Christ, inviting them to the Lord.

Some years ago I spoke for a week at a convocation in Washington, D.C., which brought together clergymen from all denominations. Shortly after I arrived in Washington I received a letter from a wife who said she was praying for her sixty-seven-year-old husband. She was praying that he might be saved at that conference and, after a service, with many tears he gave his life to Christ. The next night a young man waited for me after the service and, while on his knees, accepted the Lord as his Savior. When Sunday night came, I extended an invitation and God blessed it. Many were saved and came forward. But some of the clergymen present were highly offended in what I had done and used some harsh and critical words. A part of the program each day was a panel, and when the panel met that Monday I was called upon to defend what I had done. I was accused of conducting a cheap, melodramatic show of emotionalism which had no place in the service of Christ. I became discouraged and heavy-hearted, and I spent that afternoon as sad and blue as I could be.

When it was time for the Monday night service, the man who presided over the convocation came to my room and had a talk with me. He said, "I know that this harsh criticism has really crushed you. But we knew that it would be this way when we invited you to come, and we wanted you to be yourself. If you had not given that invitation, we would have been disappointed in you. We knew how it would be when we chose you to be the speaker for this conference. Tonight, you let the Holy Spirit lead you and do what God puts in your heart — and some of us will be praying." I felt moved of God that night to again extend an invitation, and God for the second time did as He had done Sunday night — only more responded and were saved. Following the meeting one of my critics of the night before drew me aside and apologized. He said he had never seen anything like that — for him it was a breath of heaven. I am grateful for Billy Graham if for no other reason than that on television thousands of people are seeing an invitation for the first time.

I am of the persuasion that the great purpose of the people of God is that God might use us to bring others to the saving faith we have found in our blessed Jesus. What is the purpose behind all the many activities of the church? Is it just that we keep the organization going? I know many churches that keep turning the wheels like a squirrel in a cage. It goes around and around but has no meaning, no outreach. It is like a routine we follow and, having gotten into it, we do not how to get out of it, so we go on year after year. Is that the purpose of the church? It hurts my heart just to think it could be that. The only purpose that should lie back of all the organized activities of our church is that we might bring people to the Lord.

THE SACRIFICIAL LIFE

We turn now to the sacrificial life. John speaks of the Good Shepherd who gives His life for the sheep. He lays down His life for the sheep. I do not think there is anything that God has blessed but that life has been paid for it. If it is living, it has been purchased at the price of blood. I think of our nation in this respect. When I hear and read about people who disparage America, something deep inside of me hurts. America and the freedoms and liberties we enjoy were bought for us by blood. Why, even in recent years 45,000 men laid down their lives in Vietnam. The Christian faith especially speaks of great sacrifice. In Ogbomosho, Nigeria, I stood and looked at the fine hospital, the splendid seminary, and the churches in that large city. It was glorious. But then I stood before the graves of the young men and women missionaries who were cut down at the very prime of life. They were wasted and destroyed by jungle fever and African diseases. Their lives were a sacrifice — and what a price! If we could visit the Christian churches of our country I think we would be amazed at the stories of sacrifices given on the part of many members for their individual churches. We would hear not only of the time and effort given but also of the sacrificial gifts of money and possessions.

This brings to mind an occasion that truly moved my soul. I had held a revival meeting in a strategic church in one of the greatest cities east of the Mississippi River. The pastor of that church was a gifted man. Sometime before that I had gone to a Southern Baptist Convention and had just listened to that pastor preach the convention sermon. He did it in power, and in the true spirit of Christ he blessed the thousands who were there. In a plane, riding back to Dallas, a Methodist businessman was seated next to me. We began to talk. He found out I was a Baptist minister, so he proceeded to tell me a story. In the little town where he grew up, a young girl gave birth to an illegitimate child. Since it was a small town everyone knew about it and she was covered with shame and disgrace. Having grown up in a little town, I knew exactly what he meant. Being disgraced she moved to the edge of the town and there, in a humble cottage, she took in washings and reared that little boy. The mother worked and slaved to raise her son, giving him music lessons and speaking lessons and anything else she could do for him. She sent him through high school, then kept on slaving and working in order to send him through college. He also went to seminary and became a minister. The businessman then told me he heard that the young man had become one of the great preachers in the Southern Baptist denomination. He asked me if I had ever heard of him. When he told me his name it was the person who had just delivered that powerful sermon at the Southern Baptist convention. I have since heard of the depths and reverence and love by which he took care of his mother all the days of her life. That man is in heaven now and I can believe that he shares with that wonderful mother the shepherd's crown given to those who minister to the flock.

Do these things not encourage us in the faith and in the work of our Lord? We have a great purpose and a tremendous dedication — that God might use and bless all that we have and are to the reaching and the winning of others. Does God speak to you? If He does, would you answer with your life?

CHAPTER 16

CASTING OUR CARES
ON CHRIST

1 Peter 5:5-7

Since our Lord is our chief Shepherd who watches over His sheep, He also invites us to cast all our cares and anxieties at His feet. "Yea, all of you be subject one to another, and be clothed with humility: for God resisteth the proud, and giveth grace to the humble. Humble yourselves therefore under the mighty hand of God, that he may exalt you in due time: Casting all your care upon him; for he careth for you." In this text we have a quote from Proverbs 3:34 in which we read that God resists the proud. The word used for resist in our text is *antitassō* and means to determine against, to set one's self against. It is a strong word. God *antitassō*, sets Himself against the proud. It seems unusual to us that God should take such a dislike against pride for, after all, pride is such a normal part of our fallen natures. We like to be lifted up. We like to be received. We like to be ministered to. We love being the center of attention. It is as natural to the fallen man as rushes growing by the side of a pond. When we kill it, it has a thousand lives. When we try to bury it, it bursts forth out of the tomb. It takes on a thousand shapes, and when we think we have captured it, it eludes our grasp and frustrates our pursuit.

THE SIN OF PRIDE

Pride is a God-defying sin. It flouted the justice of God as did Cain. It confronts God and challenges Him to combat as did Pharaoh — he said he did not know Jehovah so why should he obey His voice. Pride even shapes itself into a god as in the days of Nebuchadnezzar. If I understand at all, I think the Scriptures say that Satan fell because of his pride. He lifted up his spirit and wanted to be God himself. God sets Himself against pride but gives grace to the humble. Humble yourselves, therefore, into the mighty hand of God that He may lift

97

you up in due time. How do we do this? We will discuss four ways.

A man humbles himself before God when he receives the most menial office in Christ, as though it were an opportunity of great honor. The psalmist spoke of being a "doorkeeper" in the house of the Lord. This could mean just speaking a word to a little child about our precious Lord. Or washing feet. I have been in services of those primitive foot-washing Baptist people. We should do more acts of service like that in our churches today. Do little things that we might do great things. Be obedient in order that we might be rulers in His kingdom.

<h2 style="text-align:center">THE NECESSITY FOR HUMILITY</h2>

How would you depict a real Christian? How about a king keeping the door of God's house? A prince feeding little lambs? Or better still, the Son of God, clothed in the garment of a slave, washing His disciples' feet? I think that is what Peter had in mind when he used a most unusual Greek verb — *egkomboomai.* That word is used only once in the Bible and it means to bind on yourself the clothing of a slave. The garment used would distinguish slaves from freemen. I think Peter had in mind that never-to-be-forgotten moment when the Lord took off His clothes and girded Himself as a slave, to do the menial task of a household servant. There was no one in the house to wash the feet of the guests; so the Lord took off His garments, girded Himself in the clothing of a slave, and washed feet. God says that is the way to be exalted — to humble ourselves under the mighty hand of God so that He may exalt us in due time. We stoop to conquer.

We humble ourselves also by yielding, surrendering to the discipline of God. Whom the Lord loves, He chastens. And not one of us can escape the rod or disciplines of God. We must learn to receive from God's hands His disciplinary action and not fight against Him or hate Him. And a step farther — we must learn to be grateful for them. I read recently about a little boy who was very crippled. When the streetcar stopped at the corner, he called to the conductor to wait for him. The conductor kept the door open and the crippled boy struggled in and found a seat by a man who looked at the little fellow in amazement. The boy was bright, though so terribly crippled. And he was so cheerful the man could not help but exclaim to the lad, "Son, you seem so happy! How can you be that way when you are crippled?" The little fellow brightly replied, "Oh, sir, my father tells me that God always gives us what is best, and don't you think I ought to be happy with the best?" Whoever was the father of that little boy was a great man! The boy had found the answer. God gives what is best and we should receive it as from His hands so that we might be exalted. I must come to God in His way — gratefully, humbly, not arguing with Him as to how I should come but doing it God's way. I should be filled with wonder that God should love me. I am amazed that God chose me, invited me to come to Him. When God says I am to look and live, I will look. When God says I am to believe, I will believe. When God says to trust, I will trust. What does it mean to humble one's self before the Lord that He might exalt us in due time? I think it means emptying ourselves and then being filled with the divine fullness of God. Even God cannot fill a cup that is already filled. Even God cannot come into a man's heart when he is full of himself. I know men like that. They talk about themselves. They think about themselves. All of life revolves around themselves. How can God do anything for people like that? But if a man will empty himself and be filled with the fullness of the triune God, our God will exalt him in due time.

THE CHRISTIAN AND HIS CARES

In verse 6 we are told to humble ourselves under God and if we do that, we will not be burdened with the many cares spoken of in verse 7. We are to cast all our cares on Christ. There are so many things we bring on ourselves that burden us and weigh us down. They do not come from God — they are of our own making. I think of some men who are always grasping — the more they have, the more they want. The more publicity they receive, the more they desire it. The more advancement they make, the more they want to be advanced. The more famous they are, the more famous they want to be. The more money they have, the more they want to get. Such people are filled with the cares of this world and are unhappy in their hearts. They are weighed down with themselves. Therefore, I say, some cares we bring on ourselves. We are worried about the morrow, and yet God says there is enough trouble in every day we live without borrowing tomorrow's trouble. We must learn to trust God for every day.

One of the strangest things about "big" men is that they can be upset over such little things. Jonah was a great man. Jesus considered him to be one of the greatest revival preachers of all time — never had a man such a result in his preaching as did Jonah. The entire city of Nineveh, from the king down to the lowest servant, repented at the preaching of Jonah. He was a great prophet of God and a mighty revivalist. But look at him. We see him sitting on a hill, under a gourd vine, pouting. You know what he is pouting about? It started because of what God might do about Nineveh. But now he was pouting because of a gourd vine which had grown over his head, but a worm had cut it down, making Jonah angry. Not only was he angry but he also wanted to die — and all over the wilting of a gourd vine. That was Jonah, and that is so often like us. I know a man who lost his entire fortune and never thought anything about it, but he got furious with his wife over a button that was not sewn on his shirt. We become so frustrated over little things.

Spiritual Cares

Now what are these cares Peter is thinking of? There are several but one can be called a spiritual care. By that I mean we are concerned that we might not make it to heaven. What if I fall into hell? What if my soul ultimately is not saved? What is going to become of me when I die and I face the great judgment day? The Lord says to me through His inspired apostle Paul in Philippians 1 that "he which hath begun a good work in you will perform it until the day of Jesus Christ" — to the great day of His coming. In Hebrews 13:5 He says, "I will never leave thee, nor forsake thee." In John 10:28 we read His words: "I give unto them eternal life; and they shall never perish."

> What more can he say than to you he hath said,
> To you who for refuge to Jesus have fled?

Kingdom Cares

We would also like to suggest kingdom cares. Now what do I mean by kingdom cares? I mean the foreboding that sometimes fills our hearts about God's kingdom on the earth. All around us we see events and circumstances that seem to imply that the kingdom of darkness is going to swallow up the kingdom of light. One third of the earth's population is under stated atheism. Even in Christendom there is a great apostasy and a falling away of churches. Lord, what is going to become of Your kingdom? That is a care I can take to God. He presides over His own. Even on the cross when darkness tried to quench the light, it could not. I remember when I first came to Dallas I had a good talk with Mrs. Truett about her great husband, who pastored the First Baptist Church of Dallas for forty-seven years. She told me, to my great surprise, that at times the great preacher would become despondent. She said that one time when he felt he had failed, she said to him, "George, when you have prayed and asked God to bless you, and when you have done the best you can, then you leave it to Jesus." It is for us to dig the well; it is for God to send the rain and the water. It is for us to plant the seed; it is for God to make it sprout and grow. It is for us to cultivate the field; it is for God to give the harvest. It is for me to witness; it is for God to give the increase, to save the soul. When I have done the best I can, then God must do the rest, and He will.

BUSINESS CARES

I think there are also cares that attend our business life. We must make a living for our families and supply their needs. We may have staked everything we have on our business — but then we worry. That is a care I think a man can rightfully take to God. Make Him your partner. He will bless you and see you through.

Queen Elizabeth I called in a merchant in London and asked him to go on a mission for her across the seas. He would have to be gone a long time and was concerned as to what would become of his business while he was gone. He was afraid it would go bankrupt. The queen told the merchant to go and take care of her business and, while he was gone, she would take care of his. The merchant went abroad, did the work for his queen, came back, and, to his amazement, under her care and guidance his business had flourished and quadrupled. That is what God will do for you if you will make Him a partner. We find an illustration of this truth in Luke 5. Jesus had come to Peter, asking to borrow his boat for a pulpit. But Peter was a fisherman and he needed his boat in order to make a living. If the Lord took his boat He would take away his livelihood. The Bible tells us that Peter allowed the Lord the use of his boat and after He had finished speaking He told Peter to cast out his nets. And Peter caught more fish in ten minutes than he had ever caught before. Are you in a business? Make Jesus your partner. Take every problem and every decision to Him.

We can also take the cares of the home and children to Him. Does the Lord know my name? Does He know where I live? Does He know what I do? Yes, for He knows all about you and your cares and your children.

I have a magnificent painting by a Yugoslav artist, painted a century ago. It is entitled, "Forbid Them Not." In that picture Jesus is standing in a white robe. He has in His arms a little baby and children are at His feet. Peter and the others are trying to send the mothers with their children away, but Jesus stops them saying, "Forbid them not to come unto me, for of such is the kingdom of heaven." We can take our homes and our children to Him at any time. So take this care along with the rest and cast them all on Him who has bid us to come to Him. When He invites, will you come?

CHAPTER 17

DEMONS AND DEVILS

1 Peter 5:8,9

Some months ago a book and movie became the talk of the country. Both were named *The Exorcist* and dealt with a young girl possessed by an evil spirit. Peter also talks about an evil spirit, Satan himself, and his power over our lives. "Be sober, be vigilant; because your adversary the devil, as a roaring lion, walketh about, seeking whom he may devour: whom resist stedfast in the faith."

The imagery that lies back of what Peter is saying refers to a shepherd who keeps watch over his flock by night. It often happened that during the night a lion would stalk and circle the flock, seeking which one of them he could devour. With that imagery in mind the apostle uses two imperative words, each of which is translated by two words in the English. The first is *nēpsate*, which means be sober, not drunken in temperament. The second is *grēgorēsate*, and means awake, be watchful. There is no word "because" in the original and Peter goes right to the statement about the devil. In the Scriptures there is just one *diabolos* — Satan. There is one sovereign ruler over all the demons of darkness and despair and destruction. However, there are many demons, many unclean spirits.

In Revelation 12:9 Satan is called "the great," "that old serpent," "Satan," and "the Devil." Peter warns his readers that Satan is a person who walks about as a roaring lion seeking another person to devour. The Greek word is *katapiein*, which means to gulp down, to swallow down. We are told to place ourselves against Satan — the word used is *antistēte*. Therefore we are to stand firm against the onslaughts of Satan, and we are to stand firm in the faith.

We cannot understand evil in the world or in the human heart. In Revelation 10:7 the apostle John, by inspiration, tells us that when the seventh angel sounds in his day the mystery of God will be

finished. Why God allows Satan and evil and darkness in His universe
is unknown to us. Why does not the Lord, by the sweep of the hand,
or by the word of His voice, destroy all evil? Why, we do not know. It
is called in the Scriptures the *musterion* — the secret of evil which is
not revealed to us. But we do know, both in Scripture and in life, that
Satan is as a roaring lion, who encircles the flock of God, seeking to
find a person to destroy.

Satan's Beauty and Power

Let us take a look at Satan. The Scriptures tell us of the beauty of
his person. In Ezekiel 28 and in Isaiah 14 Lucifer is described as the
son of the morning. He is called perfect in beauty. I have never yet
seen a perfect anything. Everything in this world has in it some
measure of imperfection, but Satan is said to be perfect in beauty. In
2 Corinthians 4:4 the apostle Paul refers to him as the angel of light.
He is as bright as the meridian sun. In medieval days, all through
Europe, churches presented miracle plays, and in these plays Satan
was always presented in one way. He was a devil with horns, tail,
hoofs, red coat, and a pitchfork. It is manifestly a caricature, and it
may please Satan that in the imagery of the world, he was a devil like
that. Actually, he is the opposite. Satan is beautiful, alluring, and
powerful beyond anything the human mind could imagine. If I could
by illustration try to enter into something of what Satan is like, it
would be like this.

In the days of World War II, I remember seeing pictures of
beautiful women on the front pages of the newspapers. There were
pictures of alluring women in the employ of the enemy. These
women were paid to seduce a high-ranking officer to discover some
military secrets and then deliver the secrets to the enemy. That is
how Satan works. He is beautiful and seductive but also treacherous.
Satan can also be likened to the mind and voice of a brilliant and gifted
theological professor. He speaks in learnedness and eloquence, but
he denies the faith. He empties Scripture of its inspiration; he takes
away deity from Christ and makes Him just another man. He robs the
church of its hope of a glorious tomorrow. That is Satan. If I could
picture Satan as he really is, I would picture him as a great, popular
leader of government who comes forth as a champion of the people.
He soothes the people into believing he is their great benefactor and
patron. He is smart, shrewd, and deceptive, but beyond his soft
voice, there is destruction and ruin. I could go on and on and tell you
about the person and power of Satan.

In the Book of Jude the apostle writes that even Michael the archangel, when disputing with Satan about the body of Moses, did not dare bring against him a railing accusation but said, "The Lord rebuke thee."

SATAN'S REBELLION

In Revelation 12 we read about the great war in heaven. Michael and his angels fought against Satan and his angels. In that chapter we read that one-third of all the angels of God fell in rebellion with Satan. When we think of that, we wonder how it is that the angels of God turned aside from the Lord and followed Satan. But Satan is alluring. And he is also deceptive. He places his wares in beautiful order and asks us to buy them — and we do. What the angels did we do all the time. In Revelation 9 Satan is called a king and is given two other names also. In Hebrew, Abaddon, and in Greek, Apollyon, and both words mean the same thing — ruin, destruction, and death. Satan is king over all the fallen hosts of the dark and evil world in heaven and in earth, and he is also the sovereign ruler over fallen men — men who reject God. If a man will not accept the true God and worship Him, he will accept the devil and worship him. A man is made that way. He will worship something. He will follow something. Whatever we give our lives to, other than the true God, is idolatrous. It is satanic, and in Matthew 25:41 we read how Satan controls a man so completely he is sent away into the fire prepared for the devil and his angels.

SATAN AS GOD OF THE WORLD

In 2 Corinthians 11 Satan is called the god of this world. Is that not an astonishing thing? There is a kingdom in this world and it is presided over by his satanic majesty. I remember how some years ago I had dinner with Dr. Black, the president of Robert College, a Presbyterian college in Istanbul. He had married a Bulgarian and was in Bulgaria when the Communists took it over. He told me that we cannot imagine the strength and power of the Communists over their people. He said children will turn informer against their parents even when they know that what they report will mean the death of their fathers and mothers. He then added something I will never forget. He said there is a kingdom of darkness in this world presided over by a king just as there is a kingdom of light in this world presided over by Jesus Christ, and he said the kingdom of atheistic communism is an expression of the kingdom of Satan. There is a God in this world and we see Him in His illimitable power, in His command of the elements and of disease. It was Satan who destroyed God's perfect creation. It was Satan who destroyed God's recreation, and made the animal kingdom vicious and men full of murderous thoughts.

Job gives us a good example of this truth. After he had suffered his many and great losses he asked the question as to who caused his heartache and agony. He came to realize that Satan did it under the permissive will of God.

In Luke 13 we read of a woman afflicted with an infirmity for eighteen years. She could not lift herself, and the Lord Jesus said Satan had afflicted her. In 2 Corinthians 12 the apostle Paul speaks of his "thorn in the flesh," a messenger of Satan to buffet him. All of the violence you see in the world — the turbulence of nature, the stress of the wind and the storm, and the disease that afflicts us — all of this was not intended by God. It is of Satan. He is an intruder. I speak also of his power over the human heart and over the human mind. It is hard to believe how easy it is for Satan to get into the human mind and heart. He enters in a thousand ways and in a thousand forms. Day and night he circulates, seeking whom he may devour — and his ways are so deceptive.

Satan's Hold on Us

I remember attending a meeting as a little boy in which an evangelist called to the platform a big, powerful man, and sat him in a chair. He took a string and put it around the man seated in the chair and told him to break it. The man broke it easily. The evangelist then took the string and wrapped it around him three times, and the man broke it. But then the evangelist took that string and wrapped it around the man many times, and that big man did all in his power to break that string and failed. He was bound. That is how Satan works on us. He begins slowly and we do not even realize the hold he eventually has over us. He leads us as an animal to the slaughtering house. How I must war against Satan! How I must resist him! But how, Lord? Man can never find strength in himself to oppose. He is no match for Satan. Satan is too deceptive, too shrewd, and too strong for flesh and blood. We lose the battle before we begin. How does a man stand to face Satan? He does it in faith in God. Let me illustrate with Matthew 12. When an unclean spirit is gone out of a man, he walks around seeking a place but cannot find one. He then decides to return to the home he just left but finds it empty. It has been swept and cleaned. So he goes out and finds seven other spirits, more wicked than himself, and together they enter the man and dwell there. Thus "the last state of that man is worse than the first" (Matt. 12:43-45). It is not enough to just turn over a new leaf. We must thrust the spirit of uncleanness out of us, but that too is not enough. Our hearts then are empty and make easy places for Satan's demons to fill. So what do we need? We need the power of God to resist Satan's darts. We must let Jesus come into our hearts. We will then have the Spirit of Jesus, and when a man has the Spirit of Jesus in his heart, the evil spirit has no place to dwell. The Christian is in a war and it may look for a while that he is down, but he will never lose the battle. Never. All that my soul needs is Jesus. And when I have Him in my heart, He sanctifies and hallows every desire and ambition of my soul. He makes life beautiful, holy, triumphant, and finally He delivers us before the presence of God's glory without spot or blemish.

CHAPTER 18

ETERNAL GLORY

1 Peter 5:10,11

After Peter finished his sermon and exhortation he prayed: "But the God of all grace, who hath called us unto his eternal glory by Christ Jesus, after that we have suffered a while, make you perfect, stablish, strengthen, settle you. To him be glory and dominion for ever and ever. Amen." We read his prayer for those to whom he has addressed his letter. That is the way it ought to be. After the preaching comes the bending of the knee and the bowing in intercessory prayer. In Acts 20, when Paul finished speaking to the leaders of the church at Ephesus, the Scriptures tell us he kneeled down and prayed with them all.

THE SERMON AND PRAYER

Every sermon ought to be accompanied by prayer, for the minister has a twofold office. First, he is to bring to the people the whole counsel of God. He is to preach the truth of the word of the Scriptures. In Acts 10 Cornelius tells Peter that all were gathered in his home to hear the things that were commanded him of the Lord. That is why God's people gather together — to hear what God has to say. Does the Lord speak? If He does, what does He say? Thus, the first office of the preacher is to declare to the people the whole counsel of God. But he also has another office. He must pray for his people. Whereas standing before the people and opening the book in their sight is a public ministry, the minister also has a secret ministry — a private ministry. He is to bear up his people before the throne of grace in intercessory prayer. And how we need that! There is death and sickness in our midst. There are sore trials and temptations in our midst. There is a need in the soul of each of us, and the minister of God is to bear up his people in intercessory prayer.

Do you remember how the high priest was dressed when he went into the Holy of Holies? He had on a mitre and a beautiful ephod made of linen. He was beautifully decorated with pomegranates and bells, little bells so that when he went into the Holy of Holies the people could hear him and know he was there. But do you remember one other embellishment? After he was fully dressed he put on a breastplate, and on that breastplate were the names of the twelve tribes of the children of Israel. When he went into the holy place to make expiation for the sins of the people, he bore them upon his breast in intercessory prayer. That is the true assignment of the genuine pastor and preacher.

MUCH GRACE

In the prayer of our text, the apostle refers to the God of all grace. He does not say "little grace," but God is the God of all grace — abounding grace, overflowing grace, sustaining grace, saving grace, supporting grace, convicting grace, believing grace, blessed grace. He comes on our behalf to the God of all grace. That is the kind of God before whom we also come to speak, to make petition, to ask in prayer. He is a great God with abounding, overflowing grace. God gives in proportion to our asking. We are to ask, for He is a great God and is greatly able. William Carey, the father of modern missions, preached a sermon that was world famous entitled, "Expect Great Things From God, Attempt Great Things for God." Dr. Truett used to have a saying, "If God is your partner, make your plans great." It does not honor God to disbelieve Him and to think He can do only little things. We must attempt great things for Him and expect great things from Him.

There was a courtier in the kingdom of Alexander the Great who, because of personal valor and faithfulness, Alexander wanted to reward and honor. So he asked the courtier what he wanted. The man went to the treasurer and asked a great sum, so much so, that the treasurer refused to give it to him until he could first talk to Alexander. When the treasurer told the great Greek general what his courtier had asked for, Alexander smiled and said, "It is a great amount that he asks, I know, but it is not too much for Alexander to give. Let him have what he asks." Our God is like that. No matter what we ask for, it is not too much for God to give. Let us therefore ask from the God who can give abundantly. Ask that the bush continue to burn unconsumed. Ask that the barrel of meal does not waste or the cruse of oil does not fail. Ask Him and believe in Him, if you can, according to your measure of faith.

CALLED OF GOD

Peter then speaks of the God "who hath called us unto his eternal glory." I think Peter speaks of that because of the trials and suffering and martyrdom these dear Christians faced in the terrible persecution of the Roman Empire. So when he speaks of the God of all grace, he describes Him as a great God who has called us unto eternal glory.

God calls in four ways for four different things. First, He calls us to look at ourselves, to see ourselves as we really are, and looking at ourselves, we find ourselves sinful and lost and needing Him. God's second call is to look to Jesus. We are to look to Him who is able to cleanse us of sin and forgive us our iniquities. The third call is to look around us, to look at God's people, His world, and His church, and we are called to service. Each of us has an assignment and a place that only he or she can fill. We have gifts no one else has. When we carry out our assignments, the house of God is strengthened and perfected. There is also a fourth call — a final call. We are called to look to heaven. Now when we look to heaven, what are we to look for? An unbeliever would say the fourth call is nothing more than a call to darkness — a call to the grave. That final call will end in despairing dissolution and death. No man who loves Jesus and believes in the Lord could ever in the smallest beginning give himself to a belief that the final summons is a call to darkness and despair and death. The apostle calls it "eternal glory." *Doxa*, glory — the brightness of the effulgence of the iridescent God.

CALLED TO GLORY

When the Lord summons us in this last call and we are called to glory, what are we to expect? I have to confess that when I think of that, I cannot comprehend it. It is beyond what I am able to know. It is too great. For example, the apostle Paul said that he was caught up to the third heaven, and he heard and saw things it is not lawful for a man to speak about. When God calls us to eternal glory, what is that glory? Paul wrote of it again, quoting from the Book of Isaiah, "But as it is written, Eye hath not seen, nor ear heard, neither have entered into the heart of man, the things which God hath prepared for them that love him." Eye has not seen. Our eyes have seen some marvelous things. We have seen the sunset in a beautiful autumnal evening, and have seen the whole earth filled with the color and beauty of the glory of God. The Lord takes out His paintbrushes and just splatters the heavens with hues of glorious color. And there are purple mountain majesties, the rising of those snow-crowned peaks piercing the blue of God's infinite and marvelous firmament.

I could go on but let us think also of what our ears have heard. We think of the inspiring songs, the beautiful music, or the words that have brightened and gladdened our hearts. But we have not heard anything compared to what we shall hear over there. Have you ever wondered just what it is we are going to hear over there? It is beyond what any man could ever think.

Paul continues by saying neither has it entered into the heart of man the things God has prepared for those who love Him. Can you imagine that? What God has prepared for us is beyond all the beauty our minds can imagine. There are two worlds — one of them is real, and the other a world of poetic fancy and imagination. It is the world made of dreams.

Heaven, this world of dream and imagination, is not as far away as some of us might think. Nor is it surrounded by walls of impenetrable darkness, nor is it a strange and alien kingdom.

A Picture of Eternal Glory

What are some of the things of that eternal glory that God has revealed to us by His Spirit? The apostle Peter in our text names four and they are used as four verbs: *katartizō, sterizō, sthenoō, themelioo*. What do these verbs mean? Actually, *katartizō* means to mend. It is the common word for mending. In Matthew 4 we read of how Jesus, walking by the sea, called Andrew, Peter, James, and John to be His disciples. They were fishermen and He called them as they were mending their nets. So heaven is a place where God mends us, where He repairs us. We are fallen beings and we need God's mending and repairing. Some don't have eyes to see — they are blind. God will *katartizō* — He will mend. Some are bent with rheumatism; some are broken and on crutches. There are many things that happen to us in this life, but in that life God will perfect us. In that world of eternal glory, we are mended.

The second verb is *sterizō*, translated here as stablished. All the rewards in this life are transitory. They are like the great arc of the rainbow, so beautiful and colorful, but it is a tapestry of sunbeams. It is nothing but the light from the falling mist and rain — it is not established. Not so with us in eternal glory. God will set us firm; He will establish us. It will be a life that never fades away. It is a forever.

The third word is *sthenoō*, translated here to strengthen. As it is, man cannot look on God's face and live. Even the angels veil their faces in the presence of the Great Majesty. When we get to heaven,

God will enable us to stand in His presence. We will be able to do this because we will be made perfect, without spot or blemish. No wonder they say it is beyond our imagination.

The fourth verb is *themelioō*. It is the word for laying a foundation, and that is what God does for us in eternity. He sets us not on sand that dissolves, but in heaven on a foundation that is immovable. It is the foundation of the blood and atonement of Christ. We shall never be moved — never destroyed.

> How firm a foundation, ye saints of the Lord,
> Is laid for your faith in His excellent Word!
> What more can He say than to you He has said,
> To you who for refuge to Jesus have fled?
> The soul that on Jesus has leaned for repose,
> I will not, I will not desert to his foes;
> That soul, though all hell should endeavor to shake,
> I'll never, no never, no never forsake.

The promises of God in Christ are everlastingly yea and amen. It is an immovable foundation on which God has set us in Him. No wonder God's people sing and rejoice and live in victory and triumph all the days of their life, and then in glory look for the fulfillment of every sweet imagination of the heart. That is what God does for those who love Him.

CHAPTER 19

THE LIFE OF FAITH

2 Peter 1:1-4

Is your life a life of faith? Listen to Peter as he begins his second letter to the suffering Christians of his day. "Simon Peter, a servant and an apostle of Jesus Christ, to them that have obtained like precious faith with us through the righteousness of God and our Saviour Jesus Christ: grace and peace be multiplied unto you through the knowledge of God, and of Jesus our Lord, according as his divine power hath given unto us all things that pertain unto life and godliness, through the knowledge of him that hath called us to glory and virtue: whereby are given unto us exceeding great and precious promises: that by these ye might be partakers of the divine nature."

These four verses are divided into two parts. The first has to do with our faith. Peter is addressing those who have obtained like precious faith in the knowledge and in the righteousness of God our Savior. Then he speaks of the spiritual life that inevitably is a corollary — "according as his divine power hath given unto us all things that pertain unto life and godliness." And our faith and our spiritual life are the two great aspects of our holy religion. It is composed of vital, living faith that unites us to God, that gives us the nature of heaven, and of the godly spiritual life that inevitably ensues. In the Bible these are amalgamated — there is no such thing as separating the life from the faith and the faith from the life.

THE FOUNDATION OF FAITH

We can illustrate this by entering the tabernacle of old in which we find the two tables of stone, containing the Ten Commandments, written by the finger of God. This law is the foundation on which the religion of the almighty God is based. These two tables hold up that faith, and they separate the true religion from the false religions of the ancient world. So today the faith of the Lord Jesus Christ and the religion of the Bible has at its heart the spiritual commitment of the soul and life to Jesus. And those two in our most holy faith are inextricable — they are one.

The greatest sermon ever preached by Jesus, called the Sermon on the Mount, closes with these words: "Whosoever heareth these sayings of mine, and doeth them, I will liken him unto a wise man, which built his house upon a rock: and the rain descended, and the floods came, and the winds blew, and beat upon that house; and it fell not: for it was founded upon a rock. And every one that heareth these sayings of mine, and doeth them not, shall be likened unto a foolish man, which built his house upon the sand: and the rain descended, and the floods came, and the winds blew, and beat upon that house; and it fell: and great was the fall of it" (Matt. 7:24-27). The foundation is the faith, and the superstructure is the life of commitment and devotion. We build upon the great confession of our faith in Jesus Christ and the superstructure, the life of faith, is one of holiness, worship, and honor to our great and living Lord. So, we speak in this chapter of the faith. "Simon Peter, a servant and an apostle of Jesus Christ, to them that have obtained like precious faith."

Those who know me, know that I believe that every word in God's Book is inspired. It is God-breathed; it is chosen by the Holy Spirit. So when I look at the phrase: "to them that have obtained like precious faith," I see that by inspiration the Holy Spirit directed the apostle Peter to use a word that means to receive. Faith is outside of us. It is objective. It is not in us; it is something we procure. Is that true? Is that in keeping with the revelation of our Lord in the holy Scriptures? Is our faith something God must give us? Am I born with that faith? By nature, am I given to it? Do I just drift into godliness? Am I somehow saved already and all I need is just for the inward salvation that I am born with by nature to be cultivated? The apostle writes here that the faith of Jesus Christ that saves us is not in us.

How We Receive Faith

Paul wrote in Ephesians 2:8 of the receiving of our faith: "For by grace are ye saved through faith; and that not of yourselves." Our faith comes from God, lest we boast that we did it. Or look at Titus 3:5: "Not by works of righteousness which we have done, but according to his mercy he saved us." My salvation is something God gives me, and my disposition to holiness and godliness is something God does for me because by nature I am not that way. I read of a theologian recently who wrote that his nature needed to be cultivated and developed as one would weed and hoe a garden. He was saying that we are already saved. We are already in the kingdom, and all we need do is to cultivate our nature. Then he gave the illustration of weeding and hoeing a garden. I would like to tell that theologian that he can weed and hoe that piece of ground forever, but he will never have a garden. To grow a garden, you must have seed, and it must germinate and it must grow and flower and bear fruit — and that is a work of God.

To begin with, no man can make a seed. He can analyze it, he can reproduce its chemical formula, he can make it look exactly like a seed, but it is something without life. God must give it life. God makes it flower and fruit and this is what He must do for us in our hearts. Paul says in Ephesians 3 that by nature we are children of wrath. By nature we are in trespasses and in sin — we are dead. A preacher can preach to a corpse forever and it will never live. A doctor can administer all the scientific aids and discoveries but the corpse is dead forever. Only God can speak life and resurrection to a dead corpse. So it is with us who are dead in trespasses and sin. Our salvation is something from the outside. It is something God must do for us. We must be born again spiritually from above if we are ever to be in the kingdom of heaven. It is not reformation, it is regeneration. It is not cultivation, it is conversion. It is not development, it is divine intervention. Thus the faith is something that God gives us and something we obtain.

Next, Peter says our precious faith is translated through the righteousness of God and our Savior Jesus Christ. The word is *en* and that word is like our in. So let us translate it "in." As we read our text in the King James Version we might come to the conclusion there was somehow some difference between God and our Lord Jesus Christ. It has that feeling when you read "through the righteousness of God and our Saviour Jesus Christ." But Peter never wrote it that way. He wrote it: "to them that have obtained like precious thoughts with us through the righteousness of our God and Saviour Jesus Christ." It is an avowal of the deity of our blessed Lord. We see this same phrase in Titus 2:13: "Looking for that blessed hope, and the glorious appearing of the great God and our Saviour Jesus Christ." Peter and Paul have no hesitancy in avowing the deity of our Lord. They do not stumble before it nor do they draw back from it. To them, Jesus is God of very God. Whatever God is, Jesus is.

FAITH AND THE TRINITY

Now there are many who are willing to accept Jesus as a great moral teacher and a great example and a great power of spiritual strength — but not God. We have just two options regarding Jesus. He is either God as He says He is, or else He is a gross imposter, a deceiver, and a liar of the first order, for Jesus taught His disciples that He was God. The disciples worshiped Him as God, and they presented Him in the Scriptures as God. If He is not God, He is a deceiver; and if He is an impostor, He has misled His disciples into error. We who believe in Him know there is one God who has three names — Father, Son, and Holy Spirit. Tritheism is as repulsive and objectionable as polytheism. One is as bad as the other. There is one God, and His name — singular — is Father, Son, Holy Spirit. I have three names, God has three names. I have talked to people who think that when they get to heaven they are going to see three gods. There is no such revelation in the Holy Book. When you get to heaven there is one God you will feel — Holy Spirit. There is one God you will see — Jesus Christ. And there is one God who is God over all — the Father, blessed forever. These three are one. We know God as our Father, we know God as our Savior, and we know God as the Holy Spirit in us. We can illustrate this through the baptismal service. I sometimes use Matthew 28:19: "I baptize you my brother, my sister, in the name of the Father, and of the Son, and of the Holy Spirit." Sometimes I will say it like this: "I baptize you my brother, my sister, in the name of God the Father, God the Son, and God the Holy Spirit." Sometimes, "I baptize you my brother, my sister, in the name of God our Father who made us, and God our Savior who died for us, and God the Holy Spirit our great Comforter and Keeper who preserves us." We know Him in three different experiences, but the central reality is unity, not plurality or diversity.

MADE RIGHTEOUS BY FAITH

God's holiness and righteousness are imputed to us who have obtained like precious faith in the righteousness of our great God and Savior Jesus Christ. So the righteousness that we have is imputed to us — we obtain it. It is not something we possess or that we inherited by our fallen natures. When I come before God and stand before Him with my works, my righteousness, the Lord looks upon my goodnesses as filthy rags. We can never stand before God and tell Him we are worthy to mingle with the angels in glory and with the redeemed saints because of the good works we did in our lives. We can never say

we are without spot or blemish. There is not a man who can stand in
the presence of the Lord God and tell Him how good he is because
God knows our thoughts, all the secrets and compartments in our
lives, and every deed we have done. Every person, when he or she
stands before the Almighty, has to confess, "Lord, I have been a
sinner from the day of my consciousness. I have lived a life full of
blemish and mistakes. Evil has attended me and hounded my steps
every part of my earthly pilgrimage." Thus, how can a man stand
before God in that great final day? We can do it because of God's
imputed righteousness. God has given it to us.

Paul wrote of it in Romans 1:16,17: "For I am not ashamed of the
gospel of Christ: for it is the power of God unto salvation to every one
that believeth; to the Jew first, and also to the Greek. For therein is
the righteousness of God revealed from faith to faith: as it is written,
The just shall live by faith." What does that mean? The gospel that
saves us is revealed in the righteousness of God — from faith to faith.
It means that we are saved not by our righteousness, but by a
God-kind of righteousness — righteousness which is of God in Christ
Jesus. Paul wrote in 1 Corinthians 1:30 that Jesus is made to us
"wisdom, and righteousness, and sanctification, and redemption."

In Romans 10:9,10 the apostle wrote, "that if thou shalt confess
with thy mouth the Lord Jesus, and believe in thine heart that God
hath raised him from the dead, thou shalt be saved. For with the
heart man believeth unto righteousness; and with the mouth confession is made unto salvation."

In the Old Testament it was figured in type like this. A lost sinner
would take a lamb or a bullock up to the altar of God. There he would
lay his hands on the head of that innocent victim and confess all his
sins. Then the innocent victim was slain by the priest, the blood was
poured out at the base of the altar and expiation was made. The
animal took the punishment and the man, in type, walked away
washed and free. He was righteous in the sight of God. That is a type
and figure of what Christ in His righteousness has done for us. He has
taken our sins, the penalty of all our transgressions and iniquities, and
has carried them in His own body on the tree. When He suffered for
us, when He died in our place, all our sins were atoned for, paid for.
Thus I have His righteousness, His holiness, His goodness. So when
the Christian stands before God at that great and final day, he says,
"Dear God, all the days of my life I have been a sinner and I am
conscious of it and I know it. Evil and shortcomings have attended my
way. But, Lord, I plead the mercy and the love and the sacrifice of
Jesus for my sake. Lord, accept me as being holy and righteous, and

number me among those who have been redeemed by the blood of the crucified one." When a man approaches God's great judgment bar with the plea of the blood of Christ, God takes the holiness and purity of the Lord and clothes the sinner with it. This is what the Scriptures mean when they say the saints are clothed in linen pure and white.

LIKE PRECIOUS FAITH

I would also like to make a comment on "like precious faith." If you have ever taken geometry you will have been introduced to the isosceles triangle — that is, it has two sides that are equal. Peter uses the word *isotimon, iso* — equal. So Peter says we have obtained equal faith. How is it possible that I could have a faith like Peter or the apostle John or the apostle Paul? It does not mean that. It means our faith is equal in kind and structure. It speaks of its content. A small diamond and a large diamond differ only in size — the content is the same. In the ark both the small snail and the big elephant were saved from the flood. So the man who has faith as small as a grain of mustard seed is as safe as Peter or John or Paul. It is a like precious faith.

I once heard a story of a hunter up in Canada who came to a river that was frozen. He didn't know whether the ice could bear his weight, so he got down on all fours and he began to creep over that river, barely moving, thinking that any time the ice might break and he would drown in the cold waters below. While he was crawling, careful and afraid, he heard a great roar behind him. He turned his head and saw roaring out of the forest a wagon drawn by four big horses, loaded with heavy logs. The driver roared out of the forest and crossed the river. Alongside of him was that fearful man crawling on all fours. That is exactly how people are. Some of them are fearfully crawling, wondering if they will ever make it. They wonder if God will let them get five feet from the golden gate and then let them stumble so they won't make it. Their faith is so little. Then there are others who roar out of the mountains, across the river of life, and right up to the other side into the gates of glory. Actually, one is just as safe as the other. We are not saved according to the size and proportion of our faith.

Your faith may not be as robust as that of Peter; it may not be as deeply understanding and theological as that of Paul; it may not be as sweet and trusting as that of the sainted John, but if you come to Jesus by faith, you are just as saved as the apostles who leaned on His breast. What a marvelous hope and what a precious promise.

CHAPTER 20

SEVEN CHRISTIAN GRACES

2 Peter 1:5-8

In our last chapter we discussed the life of faith. But faith is only the beginning — we must build on it. "And beside this, giving all diligence, add to your faith virtue; and to virtue knowledge; and to knowledge temperance; and to temperance patience; and to patience godliness; and to godliness brotherly kindness; and to brotherly kindness charity. For if these things be in you, and abound, they make you that ye shall neither be barren nor unfruitful in the knowledge of our Lord Jesus Christ."

These verses constitute one of the most meaningful sentences to be found in God's Word. These beautiful graces, seven in number, begin with faith, then, like the scale, climb upward, ending in love. Reading this sentence in the King James Version we get the impression that we begin with faith as the bottom rung on a ladder and as we master each grace we climb up to the next one until we reach the top. That might be a possible interpretation, but as we look at this sentence, and especially in its Greek text, there is something beyond that thought. We feel that Peter is saying that the divine excellences are like a rope or like a cable with seven strands. They are intertwined and arise each out of the other. They are present in the newborn Christian when he is born into the kingdom of Christ. They are the genes of a beautiful Christian life, and as the babe grows into strength, and finally into maturity and manhood, these virtues also grow. They become dominant in the beautiful Christian life.

ADDING TO FAITH

The reason I feel this way is because of an unusual word Peter uses here. It is the word add. The sentence tells us that we are to add each virtue to the next one. Let us look at that word. It is an unusual word and also a musical word. The word comes to us from the Greek plays or dramas. The Greeks developed in their plays what they called a *choros* — a singing group. It was trained to take a part in a recitative or a beautiful song. From that word *choros* we have the word, *choregeō*, which means to furnish, to provide, to supply. That word grew out of the custom in the ancient world of the appointing of a citizen in the state by the government to supply and to train the *choros*. As time went on, the word moved away from its original meaning and was used in a general sense; so that the word came to mean to furnish or supply. It is a musical term and thus was used by Peter in speaking of the great groundwork of faith. From faith the beautiful virtues of the Christian life come. They are supplied or furnished, translated in our text as "adding."

I am intrigued by this. Following Peter's imagery, I liken the Christian life to a scale. It has a basic note, a key note, and the seven steps ascend until we come to the octave. And if the Christian life is beautifully lived, it is a song — a melody in harmony with the will of heaven.

These beautiful Christian graces, carried out in their fullness, remind me of what some of us have seen in the catacombs in Rome. As far as I know, that is the only place you will see this in Christian art or literature. On the wall of the catacombs you can see a Greek god who is depicted as a type of Christ. The person pictured is Orpheus. He is playing on his harp and around him are the wild animals in silent awe and worshipful wonder. The picture is of the young Thracian god of poetry and music. A Christian drew that on the walls of the catacombs as a picture of how our Lord subdues the violent impulses that are in us. As the animal world became worshipful and silent, so the heart of a man, touched by the hands of Christ, becomes beautiful and peaceful and gracious. This is what we see in our text.

The scale begins with the great foundation of faith which is the source of all the Christian graces. It begins with trust or committal to God. We see this illustrated in an experience the disciples had with our Lord. They were talking together about forgiveness and forgiving one another. Then the Lord said to His disciples that if a man sinned against them, they were to forgive him up to seventy times seven — in other words, they were to forgive an unending number of times. We might have thought that at that moment they would have asked the Lord for patience or forbearance. Do you know what they said? "Lord, increase our faith." Now why is that? I think it is because faith is the foundation and root of all the Christian excellences. We must remember that the Christian faith does not deal with externals apart from the great internals that give it birth. So if we have a great faith, our faith grows into a tree that bears fruit, and that is exactly what the apostle avows here.

VIRTUE

To your faith may there be furnished *aretēn* — virtue. *Aretēn* is a much-used word in classical Greek poetry and philosophy. The word speaks of moral excellence, which is fine; but there is much more in it than that. Virtue comes from the Latin word *vir*, which is the Latin for man. So virtue is manly and it refers to courage. When a man faces the confrontations and battles of life, he is to be courageous. The truly courageous soldier in a war is not without fear. His knees are shaking. His hand is not steady. His face is blanched. He is full of terror, but he enters the battle just the same. That would be a courageous soldier, and this is the meaning of the word *aretēn*. Our feet may tremble, but the rock of Christ on which we stand is immovable. We are to be courageous in the confrontation. Do not be afraid of what the future holds. Do not be afraid of the hour of death. Do not be afraid of the eternity to come. We are to face it all courageously in the faith of our Lord.

KNOWLEDGE

Then we are to add knowledge, *gnosis,* for it is possible for a person to be zealous but also fanatical. Our virtue needs to be seasoned with insight and understanding. I think it is remarkable that there is a place in the high-priestly prayer of our Lord where the Lord identified *gnosis* with salvation. In John 17:3 our Lord said, "This is life eternal, that they might know thee the only true God, and Jesus Christ, whom thou hast sent." Spiritual knowledge is a heavenly gift. It is to know that faith is the victory, that prayer prevails, that it pays to serve Jesus. What an infinitely precious knowing.

TEMPERANCE

To knowledge we are to add temperance — *egkrateia.* Often when we think of the word temperance, we think of prohibition. Actually, the word refers to that discipline by which a man is able to present himself in self-restraint, in continence before God. It is possible for a man to conquer the whole world and not conquer himself. There has never been a general that can compare with Alexander the Great. In ten short years he conquered the entire civilized world; yet he died at the age of thirty-three in a drunken orgy in Babylon.

Maybe you remember the story of John L. Sullivan, who was the boxing heavyweight champion of the world in the late 1800s. And he fought in the day when boxing was done with bare knuckles and they sometimes fought for seventy-two rounds. They fought until there was a victor. As time went on, Sullivan turned aside from the discipline of an athlete and began to waste his life in drink and debauchery. About this time a sickly young fellow by the name of Jim Corbett began to train and discipline himself for boxing. When he felt he was ready, he challenged Sullivan. Sullivan's henchmen, making the rounds of the saloons, boasted that with one blow of his fist he would pulverize young Corbett. When that battle was fought between Sullivan and Corbett it went on for round after round after round; and when it was over, John L. Sullivan lay flat on the mat. And Jim Corbett was champion of the world. Something great happened out of that and that is the reason I use this story as an illustration. When John L. Sullivan stood up, he apologized to the world for his drunkenness and his debauchery and from that day until he died he gave his life speaking to young people and to civic meetings, pleading for temperance and discipline. The eighteenth amendment, the prohibition amendment, was added to the American Constitution, partially because of the crusading of John L. Sullivan. In our lives it is a Christian virtue for a man to be self-contained and temperate.

LOVE

We are to add to temperance, patience — a bearing up under. The last three graces are a triumvirate. *Eusebeia* — piety; *philadelphia* — brotherly kindness; and *agape* — a divine type of love. I would like to spend a little time on the last — *agape*. There are three words in Greek used for love. One is *eros*, and that word came from a god of love called Eros. However, that word is never found in the Word of God. It refers to carnal love — lust — and was much used in the ancient world. The second Greek word is *philos* and this you will find in the Bible often. *Philos* refers to the love of friends. It is to love as a friend. There is another word that is used in the Scriptures, translated in the King James Version as charity. It comes from the Latin *charitas*, which means a holy and virtuous love. It is a love like God's love. It is not limited to friendship but is a love that covers the entire earth, including our enemies and those who do us wrong. *Agape* is God's love.

In the first Christian century, outside of Ephesus and on the road to Phrygia, there lived a Christian saint named Trophimus. He was said to have known the apostle Paul and the sainted John. He lived in a little cottage by the side of the road and there he humbly witnessed to the love and goodness of Jesus. He had a well of water and a bucket to draw it from the deeps in order to refresh the weary traveler with a cool drink of water. He even had bread in the house and when a traveler passed by, famished by the long journey, Trophimus had bread for the sojourner to eat. Not only that, but when eventide came and the sun was settling in the west, Trophimus had a place in his little cottage where the wayfarer could rest for the night.

One day, toward evening, down the road came three armored Roman soldiers, and they stopped at the humble home of Trophimus. Trophimus asked about their haste and journey and they replied they were under the mandate and order of Emperor Caesar himself. They had been sent on a mission to find a violent and dangerous man named Trophimus. Why? Because he was a Christian. He blasphemed, he refused to bow before the image of the Roman emperor himself. And they were sent on a mission to find him and to execute him on the spot. Trophimus told them they need go no farther. They could rest for the night and he would deliver this dangerous Trophimus to them in the morning. So he gave them drink and meat and a place for them to rest the night. While the three Roman soldiers slept, Trophimus went to his little flower garden back of his cottage home and dug a grave. The next morning, after the soldiers had breakfasted and after they had refreshed themselves, Trophimus said to them: "Come with me, and I will deliver into your hands this Christian, Trophimus." So he led them to the little flower garden and, standing by the open grave, he said, "You seek the Christian Trophimus? I that speak to you am he. I but ask that you bury me in the midst of my flowers." And he bowed his head for the stroke of the sword.

That is why in history you read that the Christians outlived, outdied, and outloved the entire Greco-Roman world. They turned it on its hinges. They changed the course of history. They remembered the words of their Savior to bless those who cursed them, to do good to those who despitefully used them, and to pray for those who persecuted them, that they might be like their Father in heaven. That is *agape* love — the love of God and the crowning virtue of the sainted Christian. How sweet will be your way, how precious your road if you will travel it as a disciple of Christ.

CHAPTER 21

THE DOCTRINE OF ELECTION

2 Peter 1:10,11

One of the most misunderstood doctrines in all of Scripture is the doctrine of election. Peter speaks of this doctrine in verses 10,11: "Wherefore the rather, brethren, give diligence to make your calling and election sure: for if ye do these things, ye shall never fall: for so an entrance shall be ministered unto you abundantly into the everlasting kingdom of our Lord and Saviour Jesus Christ." When I look at the wording of our text, I am a little surprised that the apostle does not speak of "your election and calling," which would be chronological. He turns it around and says "your calling and election." Peter does this because in life we know it to be that way. We know the calling of God, and then we learn of His predestinated election of us. You will find the apostle Paul doing the same thing in Romans 8, in the famous verse 28: "And we know that all things work together for good to them that love God, to them who are the called according to his purpose." Having spoken of it in our experience, the apostle follows it chronologically from eternity to eternity. "For whom [God] did foreknow, he also did predestinate . . . moreover whom he did predestinate, them he also called: and whom he called, them he also justified: and whom he justified, them he also glorified" (Rom. 8:29,30). From our election, we are led through our calling and justification and back to the eternity of our glorification.

TWO KINDS OF CALLING

When we speak of a calling of God there are two kinds to consider. First, there is a general call, a call of God to all men everywhere. Peter speaks of that again in the third chapter of this letter when he speaks of the delay of the Lord in His return. When the Lord ascended to heaven, He said He would return. That has now been almost 2,000 years and He still has not returned. Thus there are scoffers and unbelievers who say He has either forgotten us or He never intended to fulfill His promise. So the apostle writes later, "The Lord is not slack concerning his promise, as some men count slackness; but is longsuffering to us-ward, not willing that any should perish, but that all should come to repentance." That is a general call. It is not God's will that any man be lost, but He prefers that all men should come to repentance and to the knowledge of salvation in Christ. We see this reflected also in Ezekiel 33:11. The prophet, quoting God, says, "As I live, saith the Lord GOD, I have no pleasure in the death of the wicked; but that the wicked turn from his way and live: turn ye, turn ye from your evil ways; for why will ye die, O house of Israel?" This is a general call from God to all men everywhere that they turn and be saved.

But there is another kind of call, and that is the effectual call. It is personal, individual, and is answered by the life of the one who responds to God's call. That is a calling that comes to all of us who have come to know God in our experience. Out of God's call to the world to repentance and to faith, there are some of us who have heard that call especially and have answered with our lives. I must admit that I cannot explain, enter into, or understand the mystery of that effectual calling. Why does it bear fruit in this man's life and why does this man find himself unquickened and unresponsive? I do not know. Why is it that the same message, at the same hour, in the same place can be preached to many people and one man will be quickened so he will repent and accept the Lord, and by his side there will be another man who remains unresponsive, unmoved by it all. How do you explain that? I do not know.

I find the same thing in a family. A son of godly parents may be graciously responsive to God. His brother — of the same father and mother, the same environment, the same atmosphere, the same everything — is absolutely indifferent and unmoved. I do not understand it. It is something hid in the elective mind and predestinarian purpose of God. I just know that as I read the Word of God, and as I study it, the elective, sovereign grace and purpose of God is interwoven throughout its pages. There is no chapter without it.

For example, in Deuteronomy 7 Moses told Israel that God had chosen them to be a holy people. Then he explained it. He told them that God did not call them because they were more numerous than other people, because actually they were the fewest among the nations. But Moses said God loved them and remembered the oath He swore to Abraham, Isaac, and Jacob. The elective choice of Israel was not because of their intrinsic worth, but it was something in the mind and purpose of God.

We can also apply this truth to the individual life. In Acts 9, following Paul's conversion, God asked Ananias to go to Saul and restore his sight to him. Ananias was afraid. He said, "Lord, I do not want to see that man of Tarsus. He is here with orders to deliver us into prison and death. I am afraid of him." But the Lord told Ananias to go. "You go, for he is a chosen vessel to Me, to preach My name, My grace, My salvation to the Gentiles, and to the kings and to Israel." It is something God did. And in Galatians 1 Paul says that the Lord God separated him from his mother's womb that he might preach the gospel of the grace of the Son of God. The election, the purpose, the choice, the calling of God is throughout the Scriptures.

MY RESPONSE TO GOD'S CALL

What about our response? First of all let me say I am filled with infinite gratitude and thanksgiving to the Lord that His elective purpose and goodness reached even to me. Let me take myself as an example. I praise God's name that in His elective purpose He has placed my life in "Christian" America. I have been in the heart of Africa. I have been in villages where through an interpreter I asked an entire village if there was one Christian there, and there was not even one. Why was I born in America? I had nothing to do with it, but I truly thank Him. I also thank God that I was reared in a Christian home. I once asked my mother how old I was when she first took me to church in the little white church we attended. There were no nurseries at that time, so I asked my mother about my first visit to church. She told me she took me to church when I was a month old. How I thank God that I grew up in a household of faith. I did not choose that. There are many homes in America that are not Christian. Why was I not born in one of those homes? I thank God for His elective purpose.

I thank God for His election of a place for me to serve. There is a work God has chosen for each of us to do, and in that election I am so grateful to God. God did it, and I praise His name forever. At the end of the summer of 1944, I was eating lunch with a young man, who was a professor of missions at our seminary in Louisville and who is now the director of all our mission work in Africa. Being in school together, we had become fast friends. He grew up in Dallas where his father was superintendent of education. While we were eating lunch he asked me if anything special had happened that summer. I told him no. As the conversation continued, I happened to say that I was asked to preach in the First Baptist Church of Dallas. Dr. Truett had died and the committee had asked me to preach at the church. This surprised him and he said, "I thought you said nothing had happened." I said I still felt that way. A quarter of a century later Dr. Garner and I were once more breaking bread together. Then he asked me if I remembered that conversation in the summer of 1944.

He told me that shortly prior to that luncheon he had considered writing a letter to the pulpit committee of First Baptist Church recommending me to the pastorate of the church. He said that as he sat down to write that letter it came to him that he need not do this. It was not necessary. If God wanted me at the First Baptist Church of Dallas, he would place me there. That was why he was so interested in whether or not something had happened that summer. I was going to be called as pastor of that church. God did it.

I wish I could speak an earnest word to every young minister facing the future of the unfolding years before him. I would tell him he need not pull wires or press himself upon others for a place in God's work. God will take care of that Himself. He will open the door — the right door. God has an elective purpose for you, and if you give yourself to the will of the Lord, He will bring you into that pleasant place where He intends for you to serve.

WHAT ELECTION MEANS TO ME

I would also like to say something about what election means to us in our lives. First of all, since I believe in election and predestination, why do I not just take my ease in Zion? If God is going to do it, it will be done whether I enter into it or not. If God predestines and if God chooses and if God decides, then my entrance into it is immaterial. It will be according to what God has chosen, so why should I strive and why should I work? Now that is a legitimate question and might be a good observation of those who look at the doctrine, but when you study it you will find it the opposite. There is nothing that will get a person moving more than believing that something is God's will. God has spoken and He has elected. That is His purpose and that is my assignment. I can speak of that from history but also from experience. Do you remember Peter the Hermit? In the Middle Ages he stood up in Europe and called all Christendom to the crusade to win back from the Muslims the sacred shrines of our Lord in Israel. He was able to stir up the hearts of the Christians in Europe so they undertook the Crusades by saying "God wills it." How about Martin Luther? The day came when he stood on trial for his life before the Diet of Worms and was condemned by the Roman hierarchy. Luther, with courage and conviction, stood before that body and said, "I can do no other. Here I stand. God help me." The knowledge of God's will puts iron in a man. It makes him as steel.

Do you remember reading of the time when the Calvinistic Puritan pilgrims came to this country? They came in search of religious liberty. They came to worship God and to be free to call upon His name as they felt God led them to do. You never hear of the ultimate purpose for which they came here. They said God had called them for the evangelization of the new world and to make the new world a center for the evangelization of the whole earth. And when they came, they faced indescribable hardships that practically destroyed their colony. But they were never discouraged. God had called them.

I have a dear friend who went to a difficult place to build a little church — a lighthouse for Christ. In that community there was much bitterness against his coming, so much so that some of the citizens tried to shoot him through the windows of the church. They would take cans of garbage and, during the services, throw it down the aisle. I cannot take the time to recount the hardships he underwent as he was building the lighthouse for Christ in that place. Why did he not quit? Why did he not find a more felicitous service? Why did he not say it was too hard for him and seek an easier assignment? Because God called him to that place. He was called of God. A Christian will carry on if he feels God has called him to a particular place or work.

MAKE YOUR ELECTION SURE

The apostle also tells his brethren to "give diligence to make your calling and election sure." That raises something that I agonize through in my life. How do I know my calling and election? How do I know my assignment that I can make it sure? I want to tell you what I did and what I find so many other people attempting to do.

Through the years I sought a confirmation of my election and my calling by some kind of a heavenly sign. Lord, how do I know that I am born again, that I am a child of God, a Christian? How do I know I am in God's elective purpose and place for me? I prayed on my knees at my bedside for years and asked God to give me a confirmation. Lord, show me a sign from heaven that I am elect of God. I am ashamed to admit that I even did such a thing, but I did. And so many of us are like that. We seek to confirm our election, our calling, by some kind of esoteric experience that is alien to the mind of God, and has nothing to do with our call or election whatsoever. As the days passed I grew in grace and came to understand that this was not the way to make my election sure.

Well then, how do you make your election sure? Peter says we are to give diligence. In verse 5 he says we are to add to that diligence but we also are to add to our faith. We are to add virtue, then knowledge, then temperance, then patience, then godliness, then brotherly kindness, and then love. How do I make my calling and election sure? I work at it. I strive in it. God has called me to trust in His name and I must be busy loving my Lord, serving Him, honoring Him, praising Him. I must be diligent in it because if I am elected and called, that is the confirmation of it. When people are praising God my heart rises. I want to clap my hand or tap my foot or say Amen or do something. When the people gather on Sunday to worship I cannot conceive of my not wanting to be with God's people when they assemble to praise His name. And when God's Spirit moves in the congregation, I just overflow. That is the confirmation. And in my calling and election as a pastor, how do I make that calling and election sure? I do it by asking God to help me to be a faithful minister of Christ. Since I am responsible for the souls of my sheep — to watch over them for good, to think about them and pray for them, and to love them and to try to encourage them in the faith — I want to be a good minister of Jesus Christ.

Oh, the fullness of heart and life when we bury ourselves, immerse ourselves in the call and will of God. Is God saying something to you? If He is, will you answer, "Here am I, Lord"?

CHAPTER 22

INSPIRATION OF THE SCRIPTURES

2 Peter 1:16-21

A battle is taking place today in the Christian church regarding the infallibility of the Scriptures. Peter tells us how he feels about God's Word. "For we have not followed cunningly devised fables, when we made known unto you the power and coming of our Lord Jesus Christ, but were eyewitnesses of his majesty. For he received from God the Father honour and glory, when there came such a voice to him from the excellent glory, This is my beloved Son, in whom I am well pleased. And this voice which came from heaven we heard, when we were with him in the holy mount [the mount of transfiguration]. We have also a more sure word of prophecy; whereunto ye do well that ye take heed, as unto a light that shineth in a dark place, until the day dawn, and the day star arise in your hearts: knowing this first, that no prophecy of the scripture is of any private interpretation. For the prophecy came not in old time by the will of man: but holy men of God spake as they were moved by the Holy Ghost."

In our text Peter speaks of the sovereign glory of Jesus Christ. He says he saw His face become as the brightness of the sun and saw His garments as of the *shekinah* glory of God. Then he heard the voice of the Father in heaven saying, "This is my beloved Son, in whom I am well pleased." Peter saw with his own eyes and heard with his own ears that affirmation of the deity of Christ. But then he makes a most astonishing statement. "We have a more sure word of prophecy." What an astonishing thing to say. What Peter saw with his eyes and what he heard with his ears does not equal the affirmation of the glory and the deity of Christ that is presented in the Word of God. I am presuming that Peter might say that our eyes could deceive us and our ears might mislead us, but there is no doubt of the surety and certainty of the Word of God. In any event, it is an astonishing thing the apostle is writing here. After making that statement Peter continues: "Knowing this first, that no prophecy of the scripture is of any private interpretation. For the prophecy came not in old time by the will of man: but holy men of God spake as they were moved by the Holy Ghost."

The Content of the Word

No prophecy of Scripture is of any private interpretation. The Greek word is *idias* — which means one's own. It belongs to you — personally, individually. It is what comes out of you; it belongs to you. The word for interpretation is *epiluseōs*, which means a loosening, unloosing, a revelation. The following word is *ginetai*, which is interpreted came into being. So putting the words together we see Peter saying that there is no prophecy of the Scriptures that comes out of one's own personal disclosure. It does not originate in him. Thus the prophecy of God did not come in old time by the will of man, but holy men of God spake as they were moved by the Holy Spirit.

I think Peter was commenting on a passage he had written in his first epistle, chapter 1, verses 10 and 11. Speaking of our salvation through Jesus Christ the apostle writes: "Of which salvation the prophets have inquired and searched diligently, who prophesied of the grace that should come unto you: Searching what, or what manner of time the Spirit of Christ which was in them did signify, when it testified beforehand the sufferings of Christ, and the glory that should follow." The apostle is saying that the Word of God, describing the sufferings of Christ and the glory that should come to our Lord, came through the prophets. They delivered the message, but they could not understand the meaning. It was unfathomable to them, but they delivered God's message anyway. Thus Peter writes in our text that the prophecy of old times did not originate in man, but these men of God spake as they were moved by the Holy Spirit.

As we take another look at 2 Peter 1:20 we see that it refers to the content of the Word. "Knowing this first, that no prophecy of the scripture is of any private interpretation." Man did not originate the content of the Scriptures. It came to him by revelation. The next verse refers to inspiration — the transmission of the content. Holy men of God spake as they were moved by the Holy Spirit. Let us discuss first the revelation of the content — the substance of what is said. The word revelation comes from the Latin word *revelira* which means to reveal, to disclose, to unveil. The Greek word is *apocalupsis*, to lay bare, an uncovering. It is the removing of the veil so we can see. Now revelation has to come from God. It is divine truth that is mediated to the human messenger from God. Also, if it is a revelation, it is something man in himself could never know. It is a disclosure only God could make. If it is something man can discover for himself, it is not revelation. There are books on astronomy, chemistry, anatomy, physics, biology — all of these things that men discover and write. That is not revelation. That which comes to man by revelation is beyond him and he is not capable of ever discovering it.

THE GOD OF THE WORD

To know the God of revelation is necessary. If we are to know God it must come from a divine self-disclosure of God. No man by searching the Scriptures can find God. Man in his genius and with his telescope and all his mathematical formulas can do many things, but he cannot find God. I remember an issue of the *National Geographic* Magazine of a few years ago, in which there was a magnificent article on what our giant telescopes have discovered. We can now see the infinitude of the universe, the Milky Way, the multitude of galaxies out in space. Man can see all of this and he can make a deduction that whoever created it was omnipotent, but he can never find out who he is or what his name is. Or man can look at the beautiful sunset — the autumnal colors — when God makes the heavens show His glory. Or he can look at a beautiful rainbow or at the colorful flowers. From this he can deduct that whoever made them loved beautiful things. But he can never know Him or His name. Man can look at himself and see that he is intelligent and is morally sensitive — we have personalities. So man could deduct that whoever created us was someone of intelligence and personality and moral sensitivity. But who is He? We can never know except by a divine disclosure. Therefore we see the necessity of revelation.

Now this revelation comes in two ways. Sometimes it is given us objectively. For example, God took His finger and wrote the Ten Commandments on tables of stone. This is objective revelation. In the Book of Daniel the hand of God wrote on the plaster of the wall of Belshazzar's palace in Babylon. This is also objective revelation. Most of the time, however, the revelation is subjective. It comes from God's Holy Spirit speaking in man's soul. In the twentieth chapter of Jeremiah, for example, Jeremiah says that since God called him and sent him to be His prophet, he had nothing to say and no message to bring but destruction, disaster, and judgment, and he was not going to speak any more because the people derided him and mocked him. But in the next sentence he says God's word was in his heart like a fire in his bones and he could not help but speak. That is subjective revelation. It comes to my heart and soul, burning like a fire.

CHARACTERISTICS OF REVELATION

One of the characteristics of revelation is that it is always progressing. It goes on and on. Since it is of God and from God it moves, it is always reaching out. That is why when you see a dead church, you can believe that God is not in it, for God moves. God's creation is followed by salvation and salvation is followed by His sanctification, and His sanctification is followed by His glorification — and on and on it goes. What is latent in the Old Testament is patent in the New Testament. What is concealed in the Old is revealed in the New. There is always a reaching out and a going on.

There is also continuity in God's revelation. Genesis is a foundation that reaches toward Exodus. And Exodus is another great foundation and reaches toward the Books of the Kings. The Books of the Kings is a great foundation and reaches toward the prophets. We could carry this thought throughout all of Scripture and see the continuity of the revelation of God.

We see that God's revelation comes to us in pieces because man cannot accept but a piece at a time. He is not able to receive it all and God has to prepare us to receive His full revelation. However small the piece of revelation may be it is always congruent, it is always harmonious. For example, one could well ask if it is a revelation of God that David should have eight wives and Solomon have three hundred wives and seven hundred concubines. How could such a thing be? The Lord discusses this principle in Matthew 19 and says that man does such things because of the hardness of his heart. Then the Lord says it was not always so — it was not what He intended. Man can only take and receive what he is capable of at a certain time, but the intention of the Lord is to work toward a full revelation. The Lord said something similar to His apostles in John 16. "I have yet many things to say unto you, but ye cannot bear them now." We have to grow up and be made mature — *telios*.

God's Word came to us by inspiration — "For the prophecy came not in old time by the will of man [he did not originate it]: but holy men of God spake as they were moved by the Holy Ghost." This is how the content of the Word was transmitted to the messenger. Our word inspiration is from the Latin word *inspirari* — breathe into. The Greek word is *pneustos* — God-breathed. "All scripture is given by inspiration of God." Inspiration refers to the way the revelation was transmitted, but it also refers to how God infallibly, inerrantly did it. I must say that inspiration was necessary. If I hold in my hand the revelation of God and it has come to me with error and deception, how am I to know which is error and which is truth? Which is mistake and which is fact? Which is myth and fable and which is the truth of God? I know that today we can find many modernists and liberals who will stand in a pulpit and inform us that they can tell us what is truth and what is error. They are able to tell the difference. If that is true then my full salvation and my complete knowledge of the truth is dependent upon that man who stands in the professor's class or stands in the pulpit. I tell you that is a poor foundation upon which a man must place his soul and his eternal salvation. The truth came by divine inspiration in such a way that I can trust it and believe it — it is unmixed with error or deception or myth or fable. It is the divine truth of God. Without the divinely inspired Word I have no hope of ever coming to the truth or knowing God or being saved.

THE WAYS GOD INSPIRED HIS WORD

The way God inspired His Word is threefold. First, He did it dynamically. That is, the Lord knew the author's personality. God did not use the man as a dictaphone, but He worked through the man's personality. He used the author just as he was. Let us take Isaiah as an example. He was a man of great courage and poetic fancy. He rises in flights of oratory and poetry beyond what any genius in the secular world could ever know or achieve. To compare Isaiah with a Shakespeare or a Milton or a Dante or a Homer would be like comparing an angel in heaven to a pigmy here on earth. There is no comparison. Amos is another example. When you read Amos you smell the fresh-plowed ground. His similes and metaphors are all from the herd and flock and field. He was a country preacher, but he delivered the revelation faithfully. God dynamically used both personalities.

We see this also in the New Testament. Saul of Tarsus was a theologian. He was taught in the university and was adept at reasoning. When we read Saul, or Paul, we see a thinker, a philosopher, and a theologian of an incomparable class. When we read James we are in another world. James was the pastor of the church at Jerusalem. He spoke pragmatically, out of experience. These men were in two different worlds, but both of them were used of God — to reveal God's truth and revelation.

We also believe in the plenary inspiration of God's Word. That is, it is inspired in its fullness. That means the Bible does not contain the Word of God — it *is* the Word of God. It is God-breathed from beginning to end.

Then, the Bible is inspired verbally. God, through the Holy Spirit, inspired the writer to use the words that were used. The words themselves are inspired. The only way God can mediate the truth is by language. There is no other way, and God saw to it that the words the writer used were the words the Holy Spirit used. Let me give an illustration. I have a sermon that I frequently preach in a revival meeting. It is a favorite of all my sermons. It is based on Revelation 22:17, the last invitation in the Bible. "And the Spirit and the bride say, Come. And let him that heareth say, Come. And let him that is athirst come. And whosoever will, let him take the water of life freely." Now the whole sermon is built on the inspiration of the Word of God, for when the Holy Spirit told John to write that last invitation in the Bible, before the book was closed, He did not tell John to write "whosoever understandeth." He did not say "whosoever receiveth" or "whosoever loveth" or "whosoever feeleth let him come," but John was commanded to write, "whosoever will, let him come." If a man is willing, God will save him, forgive him, write his name in the Book of Life. Thus, I believe that the Word is inspired of God.

What happens when we believe this way? First, there is unity of authorship. In the Bible there are forty writers who wrote over a period of more than 1,500 years, but there is one author — the Holy Spirit of God. Also, when you believe in inspiration, you have unity of purpose. It reaches toward one glorious revelation, namely, that in Christ we find forgiveness for our sins, hope for salvation, and a rich inheritance which God is preparing for those who love Him. That is what God has done for us in the writing of His blessed Book. This is the inspired purpose that lies back of every verbally inspired word in the infallible Word of God.

CHAPTER 23

ANGELS AND MEN

2 Peter 2:4-9

"For if God spared not the angels that sinned, but cast them down to hell, and delivered them into chains of darkness, to be reserved unto judgment; and spared not the old world, but saved Noah the eighth person, a preacher of righteousness, bringing in the flood upon the world of the ungodly; and turning the cities of Sodom and Gomorrha into ashes condemned them with an overthrow, making them an ensample unto those that after should live ungodly; and delivered just Lot, vexed with the filthy conversation [living] of the wicked: (for that righteous man dwelling among them, in seeing and hearing, vexed his righteous soul from day to day with their unlawful deeds;) the Lord knoweth how to deliver the godly out of temptations, and to reserve the unjust unto the day of judgment to be punished."

In these verses Peter refers to the angels who left their first estate, fallen angels, who are kept in chains and in darkness until the day of the judgment of God. The King James Version tells us that God has cast these angels into hell. The word is *tartarōsas*. I want to suggest that there is yet no one in hell, nor will there be until the consummation of the age. The first to be cast into hell will be the beast. The second to be cast into hell will be the false prophet. The third to be cast into hell are the lost, those who reject the grace and goodness of God. When the believer dies, he goes to paradise, to Abraham's bosom. Some people would like to call it heaven, and that is all right; but it is not the heaven that shall be when God shall raise our bodies from the dead and soul and spirit and body are joined again. When a lost man dies, he goes to *tartarōsas*, or to torment. The unjust will be raised at the great resurrection day of the Lord as well as the just. In that day, their souls and their bodies will be joined together, and at the great white throne judgment they will receive the reward of their deeds. These fallen angels are already in that place to which the wicked go. They are in chains and darkness, awaiting the judgment day of God.

WHO ARE THE ANGELS?

Who are these angels? And why did they fall? This is a mystery God has kept to Himself. They certainly are not the devil and his angels because when Satan is finally cast out he will be cast out into the earth, and he has access to God now. He accuses God's saints day and night, and his demons are here with us, deceiving and destroying men. So, the angels in torment are not the devil and his angels, for they are free in the earth and are our accusers and deceivers. Frequently in my studying I have run across a writer who says that the angels in torment are the angels of Genesis 6 who in carnality cohabited with women in the earth, and because of that, judgment was cast upon them and they are in torment in *tartarōsas*. To me, and this is just a personal judgment, I do not feel this is the case. Then who are they? We do not know. Somehow they are the angels whom God has imprisoned, and they are in chains and in darkness and are kept against the day of judgment.

WHY ARE SOME ANGELS IN HELL?

Why are they there? What did they do? Again, this is a mystery God has kept in His own heart. He has not revealed His reason, but there is something about it that is evident. When God created the angels, He created them moral and upright and with the freedom of choice. In the ages past, given the choice of loving God or following Satan, they chose to spurn the goodness and grace of God and followed after the archangel Lucifer, and in that choice they are forever confirmed. Those who love God are confirmed in heaven, and those who reject God are confirmed in damnation. When we die, we are forever assigned to the choice we have made. If I love God and accept Christ, I am forever confirmed in the glory and fellowship of heaven. But if I reject Christ and spurn the overtures of grace and mercy, when I die I am forever confirmed in damnation and torment. These are awesome truths which God has revealed to us in His holy Word.

PRIVILEGE CANNOT KEEP US FROM FALLING

Now we look closely at our text and see some things God reveals to us. First, we notice that high office and privilege do not save us, nor keep us from falling. These lost angels were once in the presence of God, created just a little below the glory of the Lord Himself. Yet their high estate and their holy calling did not keep them from falling. Satan is wise and cunning, and his strength sours into vicious and brutal force. How astonishing that one so high, so exalted, could fall so tragically and catastrophically. We see this illustrated again with Judas. His high office as an apostle of Christ did not preserve him or keep him from the disastrous judgment that fell on him. This does not apply to our salvation, but to our ministries before the Lord. It is possible for a man to be high and exalted and yet called to the depths. That is what Paul meant when he said to the people at Corinth, "I keep under my body, and bring it into subjection: lest that by any means, when I have preached to others, I myself should be a castaway." High office and exaltation do not save us, nor do they preserve us from falling.

THE MULTITUDE OF THE LOST

Second, I find in our passage that the large numbers who will go to hell do not mitigate the awfulness of the destruction in damnation. A person cannot take comfort in the fact that millions will be there with him. What unbelievable reaching out for comfort. How is it a comfort to a man writhing in agony, in terror, and in torment, to think that there are millions of others just like him?

We can illustrate this from our text where Peter reminds us that God destroyed the world because of its sin and spared only Noah and his family. Can you picture the scene? A large population is gathered around Noah, watching him build an ark hundreds of miles from the waters to float it. They tell each other that Noah is crazy. It is idiocy that God should judge this world, that He should condemn sin. It is unthinkable. Look at us. But when the floods came and the skies were opened, what comfort would it be to a man, seeing around him the floating bodies of drowned corpses, to know that he would not perish alone? Peter mentions Lot and the story of Sodom and Gomorrah. When the fire and the brimstone fell, what comfort would it be to a man in Sodom to look around and see his wife and children and friends — everyone he has ever known — destroyed along with himself in the judgment of God?

In 1947 I journeyed through Germany. It was soon after World War II and the great masses of rubble that represented those vast cities was still there. The cities had just taken time to make a wide enough pathway through the jungle of debris for a car to drive through. What comfort would it be for a man in Hanover, standing and looking at the destruction of his vast city, to think that it was not just his Hanover that was destroyed. There is a harshness and tragedy about damnation that is inescapable and unshared. Sometimes we think that in hell we will find fellowship. From what I can read in the Bible, it is an outer darkness and the lost man is by himself — alone.

TRAINING CANNOT KEEP US FROM FALLING

I look at this passage from God's Word for the third time and I see that culture, environment, training, and background do not save me, nor do they keep me from falling. Was ever concourse more beautiful and glorious than when the angels stood in the presence of God? When the Lord God flung our worlds out into space, they sang as the sons of joy and of the morning, rejoicing in God's handiwork. They were surrounded by light, goodness, holiness, and purity. They conversed with the cherubims and the seraphims, and they stood in the very presence of God. There was nothing around them that was not holy and blessed, and yet with all of that perfect environment in which they were surrounded, they fell, deceived by the enticements and allurements of Satan. When I think of that I ask again, Can culture save us? Can training and education and background and environment deliver us? I wish that it could. Then all we needed to have done was to educate Nazi Germany and they would have been amenable to peace and righteousness. Had we done the same thing to the Italians there never would have been a Fascist party. But what about the good old U.S.A.? All we would need to do would be to educate our people and put environmental goodness around them and they would never be violent and blasphemous. Don't we wish it were that simple!

I read once about a man who had a pet leopard. One day the leopard was licking the hand of the master, and as he licked his razor-like teeth scratched the master's hand. The leopard tasted blood for the first time and immediately the ferocious nature of the animal went wild and cut its master to pieces. Underneath is always that primeval and fallen nature.

A dramatic illustration from Scripture is found in 2 Kings 8. Benhadad, the king of Syria, is sick unto death and he sends Hazael, his trusted captain, to Elisha, the prophet of God, to see if he will recover or die. Hazael stands in the presence of the man of God and asks Elisha about King Benhadad. Elisha replies, Go, tell your master he will live, but God has shown to me that he will certainly die soon. Then Elisha fastened his gaze upon Hazael, and as he looked on

him, Elisha began to weep. Hazael asked Elisha why he was crying.
And Elisha replied, "Because I know the evil that thou wilt do unto
the children of Israel: their strong holds wilt thou set on fire, and their
young men wilt thou slay with the sword, and wilt dash their children, and rip up their women with child." And Hazael looked in-
credulously into the face of Elisha and said, "But what, is thy servant
a dog, that he should do this great thing?" But he did. He took a wet
cloth and smothered Benhadad to death, and when Hazael ascended
the throne, all the violent things that Elisha wept over, Hazael visited
upon Israel. Underneath the veneer of culture and environment is
that nature we are not able to overlook.

Joseph Stalin once attended a seminary of the Greek Orthodox
Church. His mother had dedicated him to God as a priest. Out of
the righteous home of Noah came carnal Ham. Out of the home
of the man after God's own heart came the traitor Absalom. God
also said that because of the sins of Manasseh He would destroy
Judah from the face of the earth. And Manasseh was the only son of
the good king, Hezekiah. Many of you may know homes today where
the parents are godly and righteous but the children reject Jesus
Christ. It is hard to understand.

GOD'S GRACE TO THE SAVED

Oh, the grace and mercy of God that extends to us. The angels fell,
and they are chained forever in darkness, waiting for the judgment of
God. But for us God sent His own Son, our Savior. For us God made
atonement for our sins; for us Jesus died. I have sometimes wondered
why God would do that for me. Why would He send Jesus to die for
me? To make atonement in His own blood for my sins, suffer in my
stead, die my death? And the only answer I have ever been able to
find in the Scriptures is found in Psalm 103. "As a father pitieth his
children, so the LORD pitieth them that fear him," that look in
helplessness and cry to Him. He knows our frame; He remem-
bers that we are dust. God in His pity looked down in compassion
upon us and sent Jesus to make atonement for us that we might
be saved.

A man had two sons. The older son was in college, a star athlete, a
handsome specimen of young manhood. The father also had a
younger son, and the little boy gave promise of being as fine and as
strong as his older brother. One day, in some unexplainable accident,
the little boy got tangled up with his bicycle and the wheels of a big
truck. In the hospital the doctor turned to the father and said, Sir, the
only way I can save the life of the boy is to amputate his left arm and

his right leg. The father said that as he looked down into the face of his little boy, he knew for the first time what the Scriptures mean when they say, "As a father pitieth his children, so the LORD pitieth them that fear him." I thank the Lord for His goodness, His grace, and His mercy that comes down to those of us who greet Him with open arms and with open heart.

CHAPTER 24

THE PROMISED COMING

2 Peter 3:1-4

There is no subject mentioned in the Bible more frequently than that of our Lord's return. Peter also writes of this to the persecuted Christians of his day. "This second epistle, beloved, I now write unto you; in both which I stir up your pure minds by way of remembrance: that ye may be mindful of the words which were spoken before by the holy prophets, and of the commandment of us the apostles of the Lord and Saviour: knowing this first, that there shall come in the last days scoffers, walking after their own lusts, and saying, Where is the promise of his coming? for since the fathers fell asleep, all things continue as they were from the beginning of the creation." Peter was martyred about 30-35 years after Jesus' ascension. And if he thought there were scoffers in his day questioning the promise of our Lord's coming, what would he say today after 2000 years? The scoffers said everything continued as it was from the beginning of creation. They could not see any heavens rolled back like a scroll. They did not see Jesus coming down out of the sky. What about that promise?

THE PAROUSIA

The term "second coming" itself cannot be found in Scripture. It is always referred to as the *parousia*. *Para*, like parallel, means alongside. *Parousia* means the coming alongside. Actually, the word means the presence of the Lord — the coming of the Lord to be alongside us throughout life. There is no event comparable to it in all of time, and this doctrine is interwoven in the warp and woof of the Christian faith. At the center of our Lord's teachings we find in great detail a discussion of the circumstances of His return. We read of this in His apocalyptic discourses in Matthew 24 and 25, and in Mark 13 and Luke 21. We see this referred to also in our Lord's parables. We find the parable of the wicked servant who, because the Lord delayed His coming, became drunk and riotous and began to beat his fellow servants. We see it illustrated in the Lord's story of the five foolish virgins (or bridesmaids) and the five wise virgins. The Lord delayed His coming and the five foolish women let their lamps run dry because they did not plan on a delay. We find it in His story of the parable of the talents. To us a talent is a gift. In the Scriptures a talent is a money weight, like a shekel is a money weight. In that parable we read of how the man used his stewardship until the Lord returned. The same holds true for the parable of the pounds. The main characters in these parables were to use the pounds for God until He came, at which time they were to give a reckoning of all they had and all they did for the Lord. We must apply this same truth to our lives.

Then in our Lord's parable of the sheep and the goats we read that when our Lord returns, He will divide those who are saved from those who are lost. Now the wheat and tares are growing together but not forever. That great day is coming when Christ will return and we will stand before His bar of judgment as He divides the sheep from the goats. This is all involved in the teaching of our Savior concerning His return.

THE LORD'S KINGDOM

When our Lord asks us to pray "thy kingdom come," it is a prayer for the return of our Savior — "Lord, come quickly." John speaks in the fourteenth chapter of his gospel of our Lord's coming again. Paul mentions it in 1 Corinthians in the memorial of the Lord's Supper when he said, "as often as ye eat this bread, and drink this cup, ye do shew the Lord's death till he come." The truth of our Lord's return is found also in the preaching of the apostles. Luke, the beloved physician and amanuensis of Paul, begins the story of the apostles in the Book of Acts with these words. They asked the Lord, "Lord, wilt thou at this time restore again the kingdom to Israel? And he said unto them, It is not for you to know the times or the seasons, which the Lord hath put in his own power. But. . . ." Then he gave them the promise of the Spirit, and while they were talking to Him He was raised upward and out of their sight. And the *shekinah* glory of God hid Him away. As the disciples were transfixed, looking up to where Jesus was caught away in the glory, an angel tapped them on the shoulder and said, "Why stand ye gazing up into heaven? this same Jesus, which is taken up from you into heaven, shall so come in like manner" — in the same *shekinah* glory.

Revelation 1:7 also tells us He will come in the *shekinah* of God — the iridescent garments of the Almighty. He is coming back just as He left. That is the way the story of the Acts of the Apostles begins. The writings of Paul to the Thessalonian Christians, Peter's letters — all mention the coming of our Lord. Because of His coming we are not to quake under affliction and persecution. And because of His coming we are not to sorrow as others who have no hope. The whole fabric of the Christian faith is held together by that incomparable promise — the return of our blessed and living Lord.

THE SCOFFERS

Scoffers are still with us today who say, "Where is the promise of his coming?" Actually, the scoffers say there is no hope of any such day as that. No return of our Lord is to be realized. And when they do try to accept somewhat the promise of the return of our Lord, they spiritualize it and rationalize it. There is to be no actual coming. We are never going to see Jesus, and this world will never be renovated, made new. They say there has always existed in the heart of man a hope of a new day and a better tomorrow. It is nothing but a reflection of that hope for something better that never dies in the human heart. It is just a dream. They substantiate it by a satanic doctrine that has come to be universally accepted in the academic world — Darwin's theory of evolution. This theory says we are evolving and evolving, getting better and better, and we are going upward and upward. This is the only utopia, the only heaven — this is the only second coming of Christ we will ever know. It is all in the progress of the human race. They say that the time is coming when the tiger and the ant will be bred out of us — when evil will disappear from our midst. They say that sin is nothing but the drag of our animal ancestry. Give us time, and we shall evolve — progress — into angels, and maybe some of us into archangels.

A tragic fact is that many men of the cloth in this modern day scoff at the return of the Lord and also question the promise of His coming. I quote from one of the great theologians of this century: "To bring Jesus into the control of human affairs is the real coming of the kingdom of God upon earth. This is what the pictures and the apocalyptic symbols used by the early Christians really meant. This is the real coming of Christ — the control of human affairs by the spirit of Jesus." I also quote from one of the great preachers of all times who lived in this century. This great preacher said: "When they say Christ is coming, they mean that slowly it may be but surely His will and principles will be worked out by God's grace in human life and in human institutions. You're never going to see Jesus. There will never be a personal return."

THE DESPAIR OF EVOLUTION

Just look at those statements for a moment. It is this kind of doctrine that has given birth to the cynical despair called existentialism which has plunged this modern, intellectual world into indescribable hopelessness and grief. There is no way out. There is no hope. There is no light beyond the grave, at least not to modern philosophers. Just when man thinks he has advanced, he finds he has fallen into a worse situation. He faces one problem and solves it only to find that a worse problem confronts him. We as a nation can look back through the years and find many problems faced and overcome, only to discover something far more serious has taken its place. And it will always be so until Christ comes again. What could an evolutionary progress of the human race do to ameliorate the hurt and suffering of an earthquake such as that experienced in Guatemala? What can it do to feed the millions of starving people? What about death? If by pills and vitamins and scientific advancement we someday might live to be 200 years old, we still face that grim enemy —death. What could I hope for in inevitable progress in evolutionary achievement? For what could I hope for those who have already died? Do we have to leave them in the cemetery forever? Does that sound like God? Does He forget the least of His saints who looked in trust to Him? Does God lie when He says He is coming back? He promises so much to those who look in faith to Him. Are these promises worthless? Has God deceived us? Has God misled us?

THE LORD IS FAITHFUL

My brother, my sister, a blessed fact of the Christian faith is that the Lord is faithful, and He will keep His promises. No word He has ever said to us by His Son shall ever fall to the ground, but the promises of God in Jesus Christ are everlasting and amen. And when God's Word says He is coming, be ready. When it says He is coming, dry your tears. When it says He is coming, do not live with a broken heart. When it says He is coming, victory is in His hands. Lift up your head, lift up your faces, dry your tears, be ready for the shout, ready for the glory, ready for Christ. He is coming again. This is the promise of God; therefore, the Lord tells us to lift our heads, for our redemption draws nigh. He is on His way. I can hear the trumpets sounding — I can almost see His face. He is coming!

CHAPTER 25

THE WORLD ON FIRE

2 Peter 3:5-13

In our last chapter we discussed the second coming of our Lord. Along with this great event Peter tells us of the destruction of this world. "There shall come in the last days scoffers, walking after their own lusts, and saying, Where is the promise of his coming? for since the fathers fell asleep, all things continue as they were from the beginning of the creation." With sarcasm in his voice the scoffer is saying, "I don't see any change. You say the clouds are going to receive Jesus, but I don't see any clouds coming for Him. You say the heavens are going to be rolled back like a scroll, but I don't see any heavens rolled back like a scroll. And you say God is going to call us into judgment, but I don't see any calling to judgment. Everything is going just as it did from the beginning of the creation."

Without realizing it, he hides his face from the words of Peter: "That by the word of God the heavens were of old, and the earth standing out of the water and in the water: whereby the world that then was, being overflowed with water, perished: but the heavens and the earth, which are now, by the same word are kept in store, reserved unto fire against the day of judgment and perdition of ungodly men. . . . But the day of the Lord will come as a thief in the night; in the which the heavens shall pass away with a great noise, and the elements shall melt with fervent heat, the earth also and the works that are therein shall be burned up. Seeing then that all these things shall be dissolved, what manner of persons ought ye to be in all holy conversation and godliness, looking for and hasting unto the coming of the day of God, wherein the heavens being on fire shall be dissolved [loosed — the whole world just coming apart — whatever holds it together just dissolves], and the elements shall melt with fervent heat? Nevertheless we, according to his promise, look for new heavens and a new earth, wherein dwelleth righteousness."

SCOFFERS AT THE LAST DAY

It is easy to see what happened in Peter's day because the same thing happens today. At the time Peter wrote this letter the people who did not believe in the Lord had heard the preaching of the gospel. They had scoffed at it and walked after their own fashions and after their own lusts, and said, Where is God? Is He out there somewhere? If He is, He is certainly not here. Where is the promise of His coming? That is just preaching — it is just so many words. They then deduced that if there was no God and no judgment and no intervention from heaven, then they were free to do as they pleased. So they followed their own lusts and gave themselves up to their own carnal desires. You would almost think Peter was writing today. Promiscuity and permissiveness characterize our modern society. We live today as though there is no God and act as though everything goes on as it always has. The earth turns on its axis and the phenomena of sunrise and sunset goes on just as it always has. But the apostle, writing of that day and by prophecy characterizing our day says this deduction is wrong. He says we think that because everything continues as it has, God does not intervene in human history.

Peter gives an example of the intervention of God in human history to prove us wrong. It is taken either from Genesis 1:1 or Genesis 6, depending on which commentary you read. If the reference is to Genesis 1:1, then Peter is referring to the destruction of the world by water, when sin was found in Lucifer and one third of the angels in heaven. When this sin was found the created work of God dissolved. Sin always curses and destroys, and it did also in the beginning. When God created the heavens and the earth, He created them perfect. It is impossible for me to imagine God doing an imperfect or ugly thing. God made the world and the heavens perfect, but when sin was found in it, sin destroyed it. The Scriptures say that our earth was a chaotic mass with water everywhere. Following that chaos the Spirit of God moved over the face of the deep and God separated the waters — some went into the clouds and some below. Then God separated the waters below and the dry land appeared, and the water was gathered into great ocean beds — but the first world was destroyed by water.

GOD IN HISTORY

There are other commentators who say that the illustration the apostle uses here of the intervention of God in history refers to the day of the Flood. Imagine that picture! The mockers in that day looked at Noah and said he was crazy. Who would build an ark 150 miles from enough water to float it? But Noah preached for 120 years and for 120 years men mocked and ridiculed and made fun of Noah, but the judgment of God came and God did intervene. Just as Peter's example here of the destruction of the world by water, we can see often the intervention of God today. God is not out there somewhere. He is here and He is not oblivious to what we do. God knows and He intervenes and He judges. Peter also could have used the judgment of God in the days of Sodom and Gomorrah when the cities were burned by brimstone and fire. He could have used the illustration of the intervention of God in the days of Assyria.

Does God intervene in human history? He did in 587 B.C. when the temple of Solomon and the holy city were completely destroyed and the people carried away into Babylon. He did in A.D. 70 when, under Titus and the Roman legions, Jerusalem was destroyed. Does God intervene in human history? We see that He does often. We could tell of God's great wind as it destroyed the Spanish Armada. We could tell of the snowstorm in 1812 that beat Napoleon. We could tell of the Lord looking down on Nazi Germany and Hitler and saying, It is enough. He reached into His box of damnations and sent bombs and fire upon the vast cities of Germany until they lay in ruin and in rubble. Does God intervene? Does God judge?

What About America?

When I think of those scenes and take a good look at America, it frightens me. God has blessed America these past two hundred years. As I review our nation's history I cannot help but think of what our forefathers went through to fashion the fabric of our country. They built churches and Christian schools, preached the gospel, called men to repentance, and built our nation on the love and mercy of God. But today we are in the process of dissolving the fabric of this nation, and God's longsuffering watches us. I suggest that if America does not turn from her evil ways, God may again open His box of damnations to chasten and scourge us as a people.

Aspects of the Judgment

Our text, by revelation, tells us that God is longsuffering and is not willing that any should perish, but that all should come to repentance. Peter reminds us that in God's schedule a day is as a year and a thousand years as a day. The time of God's judgment will come as a thief in the night, that is, unheralded. It does not mean that God does not speak of it and tell us about it. When men say there is no such thing as God's judgment, no intervention from heaven, then it will suddenly come. And when it comes, Peter says that this very world will pass away with a great noise and the elements shall melt with fervent heat. What an awesome revelation that is. God does not fill in the details in much that He discloses to us, but He always reveals to us the future. The Lord tells us that we are hastening to a great rendezvous, a great judgment day with almighty God, and in that awesome day this world will be judged by fire as it was judged in generations past. Historians have had much to say about it. In fact, Pliny the Elder, in the first century, wrote that it was a miracle the earth escaped burning by fire any day. You would think that Peter was a chemist because of the way he writes. He says this earth will pass away with a great noise, a great explosion, and the elements shall melt with fervent heat. Peter could not have known at the time he wrote his epistle that every element is subject to melting. There are about one hundred different elements and every one of them can be melted. Each can be reduced to liquid and finally to gas. The ocean can be used as an example, for it is made of hydrogen and oxygen and both are highly combustible.

I remember in my chemistry class in high school our teacher illustrated this for us. He took a beaker and placed in it a vial of hydrogen. He added a vial of oxygen and then put a match to it. It made a great explosion, and when we opened the container and looked in it, we saw that only a drop of water was left. Our world is covered with oceans and seas of water, made of highly combustible material. When we see something burning we say it is on fire. Actually it is just oxidizing. It is the union of oxygen with whatever elements are in that article that is afire. All God has to do is to speak the word, and His elements become a flame of fire.

Geologists also have something to say about this. They say the earth is like a globular egg, and the shell is comparatively the same proportion to the egg as this cool crust is around a molten and liquid lava-like core. The earth is melted on the inside, in fervent heat. If you go down into the earth it begins to get hotter and hotter until finally the great pressure of the weight upon those elements underneath make it liquid. Once in a while a little valve will open and we see the eruption of a volcano. We literally live our days upon a burning mass of molten lava, and the geologists say the turning of the earth has flattened the poles about thirteen miles on each end. That is the kind of world in which we live, and God would have only to break the crust of the earth and all would burst into a molten mass.

The astronomer also adds his picture. He looks up into the heavens and finds exploding stars and burned-out spheres through great galaxies. The Scriptures tell us that when that awesome day comes the moon will turn to blood red and the sun will be shut out in darkness like sackcloth of ashes. I think this means that when the moon turns blood red it is a reflection of the burning of the earth. The shadows of the burning fire make the moon look red; and when it says the sun is darkened like sackcloth of ashes, I think the fire and the smoke of the burning air shuts out the very sun itself and it turns dark. What a day that will be when God makes His final intervention in human history.

When will that be? I think it is easy to find out when that day will be. Peter says it is going to come to pass in the day of the judgment of ungodly men. In the Revelation I read that when the ungodly men who refuse the overtures of grace and mercy of our Lord Jesus stand at the great white throne judgment, the earth and the heavens will flee away and there will be no place for them to hide. That is the great judgment by fire. And each day all creation is moving closer to that great rendezvous. The astronomer tells us that our universe is moving through space at a terrific pace. Moving toward what? It is moving toward that great judgment day of almighty God. We read the annals of history and find that the great social orders and political mechanisms of this earth are moving. They never stand still. Where are they moving? To the great judgment day. And our lives are also like that. We are moving. The rich man in his limousine is riding to that judgment day. That poor man barefoot and in rags is walking to the day of judgment. That young man with fast step is moving toward it. And that old, feeble man on his cane is tottering to God's day of judgment. Even the little child who reaches his arms up in the crib is reaching to the judgment day of almighty God. The Christian and the lost sinner will both stand someday before the judgment throne, and when that day comes for both the lost and the wicked, that is the day of the dissolution of the earth and the heavens by fire.

THE MELTING OF THE ELEMENTS

I would like to add a word as to what Peter means when he says that these elements shall melt with fervent heat and what John means when he says the heavens and the earth will pass away. There are learned commentators and Bible scholars who avow that this means the absolute destruction of this whole earth and the whole universe above us. They say it refers to annihilation. They feel God will destroy all that exists, and then He is going to make everything new again. Now, I have no quarrel with the exegetes who say that, but my opinion is different. I have studied the Book of Revelation for two years and I just do not feel it means the annihilation of matter and the destruction of this world or of the heavens about it. I think it refers to a rejuvenation. I do not think matter can be destroyed. I think matter has the character of God in it. You may take a match to something and it may look burned up but it has just taken on another form. Every atom and every molecule that was in the beginning is still in existence. Some of it may turn to vapor, some to smoke, and some to ash, but it is still there. Matter is indestructible — it has the character of God. It is forever. I think that the new heavens and the new earth mean that God is going to purge the heavens. There will be marvelous new heavens above us and there will be a marvelous new earth on which to stand. It will be this earth, but it will be purged by fire. It will be those heavens above us, but they will be cleansed.

The New Heavens and New Earth

Today everything is cursed but there is coming a time when God is going to cleanse all and there will be a new heaven and a new earth. There will be the new Jerusalem coming down from God out of heaven. The Lord is building it up there in that third heaven — the great, beautiful home for His people. He says, "I go to prepare a place for you. And if I go . . . I will come again, and receive you unto myself." He is building that beautiful home in heaven called the new Jerusalem, and when the earth is renovated and when the heavens are made new, that beautiful heaven will come down from God and rest here on this earth, and this is going to be our heavenly home — a new day, a new earth, a new heaven, a new home, a new body, a new and precious fellowship. God shall wipe away all tears from our eyes and there will be no more death, neither will there be sorrow nor crying nor any more pain, for all these things will have passed away. To think what our eyes some day will see in that majesty and glory! That is why God's people do not have to be afraid. The whole earth may be judged by fire but for God's people there is no fear, no dread. We hasten to the coming of the Lord and the day of our Christ. The words that are written in God's Book were written for our comfort. In that day not a hair of our heads will be singed, nor will the smell of smoke be found on our garments. God's children will be with their Savior in glory — saved forever. Therefore we should praise God and lift up our voices in gratitude and thanksgiving. Even so, Come, Lord Jesus! You know my heart — I am ready! I have made my peace with heaven. I have given my heart to Christ. Have you?

CHAPTER 26

THE TIME ON GOD'S CLOCK

2 Peter 3:8

In our last chapter we discussed verses 5-13 of this third chapter of 2 Peter. In this chapter I would like to take out of that passage verse 8 and spend some time with it. "But, beloved, be not ignorant of this one thing, that one day is with the Lord as a thousand years, and a thousand years as one day." In my preparation for this chapter I came across many interpretations of this text. It is a famous one and is preached often — a thousand years as a day and a day as a thousand years.

This text can be interpreted either spiritually or literally. I remember a message from a great preacher of the past who spiritualized it. He found in it hidden esoteric meanings that belong to one's experience. He said that this text referred to man's human experience in which he goes along in the same way year after year. Suddenly a great crisis appears in his life and in that one moment all of life thereafter will be changed. For a thousand years there is no change; then a great crisis comes and a day is as a thousand years.

We can illustrate this from a recent experience. Some time ago a man from the Pentagon appeared before the Senate committee on armed services. He pointed out to that committee that Russia is presently building such nuclear weapons as to be able to annihilate the U.S. in one moment — in one surprise attack. That would illustrate what this preacher was talking about. Our country could go along a thousand years as a day, then suddenly a day would be as a thousand years, in which with one catastrophic nuclear attack the whole nation could be wiped out. I do not have any objection to that spiritualization because that is good preaching and a good message. Our lives are sometimes like that. Suddenly in our everyday lives something happens and life is never the same for us.

WRONG INTERPRETATIONS

There is an interpretation of the text I do not like, however. Some like to take the passage and use it to set a day for the coming of the Lord. For example, one took the passage in Hosea 6. In that chapter the prophet says "Come, and let us return unto the LORD; for he hath torn, and he will heal us; he hath smitten, and he will bind us up. After two days will he revive us: in the third day he will raise us up, and we shall live in his sight." To this interpreter the Resurrection is the coming of Jesus. The text says "in the third day he will raise us up." So, if a thousand years is as a day, it will soon be 2000 years — two days — since Jesus has gone. And in the third day, after A.D. 2000, He will come back and we shall live in His sight. That is interesting. I would not have any objection to that except I do not think it is true.

Another way in which some expositors set the time of the coming of the Lord from this text is to go back to Genesis 2. The heavens and the earth were completed and all in them. On the seventh day, following the days of creation, God rested from all His work. So there are six days of God's creation and the seventh day is the Sabbath day of rest. Now some expositors take those days and refer to Hebrews 4:4-6. These verses speak of God resting from His creation and verse 9 says, "There remaineth therefore a rest to the people of God." These expositors take this text which says that a thousand years is as a day and after six days comes the Sabbath rest. So after six days — 6,000 years — will come the next millenium, the seventh one, and that will be the final rest for the people of God — the coming of Christ and the establishment of His kingdom. I cannot accept this interpretation, but I use these two interpretations as an illustration. So much of the preaching and writing concerning the Word of God is like that. It is taking the verse or verses out of context and does not give the meaning of the inspired apostle.

CLING TO THE FAITH

What is it that Peter was talking about when the Holy Spirit inspired him to write these words? First of all he tells us that the fact that one day is with the Lord as a thousand years and a thousand years as a day must not be hidden from us. There are two things about which he is writing. First, he is writing about the scoffers who question the promise of His coming. To them the world has gone on as it has from the beginning of the creation and it is no different than when their fathers died. So Peter says to the scoffers that a day is as a thousand years and a thousand years as a day with God. God may delay His coming, but God's clock is not like ours. Also, Peter is trying to encourage us to cling to the faith and not give up. The Lord is coming, though He tarries. Our clock may go fast but God's clock may not be like ours and His time may not be congruent with ours. We are not to be helpless and hopeless in our waiting for the great consummation of the age. The Lord is coming!

Let me give you an illustration from Paul. When Paul and Silas preached at Thessalonica, the capital of the ancient province of Macedonia, they preached of the coming of the Lord. Then, as you know, persecution drove Paul and Silas out of Thessalonica and they went down to Athens and then to Corinth. While they were gone, some of the beloved saints in Thessalonica died. So the church sent Paul a letter saying they were looking for the Lord. They were expecting the return of Jesus, but He had not come, and while He delayed His coming, some of the beloved brothers and sisters had died. What of them? Would they share in the kingdom, or was it over for them? Did they miss it because the Lord had not come?

In answer to that question Paul wrote 1 Thessalonians from Athens and 2 Thessalonians from Corinth. He told them that the dead in Christ would rise first and then those who were alive and remained would be raptured — would be caught up with the Lord in the air. Thus, we are comforted and strengthened in our waiting for the delayed return of our Lord, for, says the apostle, God's clock is different than our clock. On God's clock, a thousand years is as a day and a day is as a thousand years. There is no time with God. Time is the creation in which we are imprisoned, but not God. To us, if a thing is near, it could be five minutes from now or an hour from now. That would be near. And to us if a thing is a thousand years from now, it is far off. To God there is no near or far. It is all just here — present. God has said His name is "I AM." He did not say His name is "I was," as though there was change or development in God and He is not what He used to be. And He did not say His name is "I shall be," that is, there are other things to be in the life of God that are yet to be reached for. No. He says His name is I AM — I AM in the past, in the present, and in the future. He is always the same and always is present with God. To us, things happen a day at a time, but God looks upon all of it in the present — the Lord looks at it all from the beginning to the end.

THE ENTIRE PICTURE

Some time ago I took a canoe trip with one of my deacons down the Illinois River in the Cookson Hills of eastern Oklahoma, one of the most beautiful streams in the world. The river twisted and turned, and around each bend we saw things happen one at a time as we came to them. But you could stand on the top of one of the highest hills in the area and could see that river for a long distance. That is how God sees things. To us, things happen one at a time, a day at a time, and we do not know what is around the bend of the day. But God sees the entire picture from beginning to end.

GOD'S TIME

Our text says we are not to be ignorant of this truth. Some people willfully hide their faces from the truth of God and some of us do it in neglect, and I think in this verse Peter is speaking primarily to the scoffers. This is the person who laughs at the promise of His coming. They don't see any heavens rolled back like a scroll and they don't see any Lord Jesus Christ coming down from above. All they see is the world in which they live. They scorn the Christian faith and the Christian promise. They laugh at the idea of a mighty Lord who is its history, its destiny, and its consummation, and who is coming again. I think such people are like the molecules that thrive in a little drop of stagnant water. Maybe when you went to school, you took a microscope and looked at those thousands of amoebas and paramecia that were swimming in that little drop of water. That is a fascinating sight, isn't it? You could have millions of these creatures in one drop of water and you would still have only a drop of water. Any one of us could take that drop of water and break it into many drops. Such are the philosophers and scoffers of the world. Though there may be millions of them in the world, God can scatter them and destroy them. They are just drops of water in the vast ocean of God's infinitude. They are like grains of sand in the immeasurable seashore of God's existence.

I remember an experience that happened when I was a teen-ager. Sinclair Lewis, the famous novelist and agnostic, was living at that time. One day Lewis stood up in a pulpit in Kansas City and made fun of the idea of God. He said, "If there is a God, I challenge Him to come and strike me dead here in this pulpit." And when Lewis said that, the whole world of infidelity applauded. How smart! Man, did you ever hear anything like that, said the whole world? They headlined it in the newspapers and wrote of it in editorials. How well I remember that. I also remember that at that time many of our newspapers carried a column entitled "Today" written by Arthur Brisbain. Brisbain wrote about Lewis and his statement from that Kansas City pulpit. He said Lewis reminded him of a little ant in the

deserts of Arizona. Through the middle of Arizona ran the great Santa
Fe railroad. This little ant got on top of one of those big steel rails and
lifted his hand and said, "I am told that the head of this railroad is a
man named Charles Storey. I don't believe it. If there is a Charles
Storey who runs this railroad, I dare him to come out here to Arizona
and step on my head." Then Brisbain said Charles Storey would say,
"It is just not worth my time." Right! Why should the almighty of the
universe, the sovereign God of time and eternity take time out to
come to earth to strike down Sinclair Lewis?

I think this is what Peter is talking about. Our little world and our
little clocks and our little timepieces — how we watch them. Not
God. To God a thousand years is as nothing. He may delay — to us He
tarries — to Himself, His judgment day is on time.

Why does God delay at all? Why does God not judge the world?
Why does He not stamp out evil? Why does God not do something
about those who plan war? Why does He not come? He says He is
waiting that we might be saved. He is hoping that someone will open
his or her heart and accept His great salvation. After the passing of the
years the Hallelujah will be sweeter, and the triumph will be greater,
and we will rest in that fair and happy land by and by. He is coming —
He is on the way. It may seem long to us, but we must remember
there is no time with God. He brings with Him infinite goodness and
grace and blessing for those who look in faith, in love, in acceptance to
Him. Look to Him now. Accept Him now. The blessing is forever —
it never fades away.

CHAPTER 27

LEST ANY PERISH

2 Peter 3:9

"The Lord is not slack concerning his promise, as some men count slackness; but is longsuffering to us-ward, not willing that any should perish, but that all should come to repentance." What a beautiful thought. God does not desire that any should perish, but that all should come to repentance — that all should be saved.

BACK TO THE SCOFFERS

Let us go back for a moment to those scoffers mentioned in verses 3 and 4. I suppose it is a good question these infidels ask — Where is the promise of His coming? You say the Lord is coming back to this earth? Well, it has been a long time and we have not seen any such development.

I do not think there is any doubt but that the Christians who lived in the first generation confidently awaited the coming of the Lord in their day and in their generation. They were taught that. The conclusion of the great apocalyptic discourse of our Savior in Matthew 24 says: "Watch therefore: for ye know not what hour your Lord doth come." The Lord Himself prepared His disciples for His imminent return. When the Lord was taken up into heaven and the *shekinah* glory received Him out of their sight, the disciples stood transfixed, looking up into heaven. The angel came to them and said, "This same Jesus, which is taken up from you into heaven, shall so come in like manner as ye have seen him go into heaven." They were to expect the return of the Lord and they were taught the imminency of His return. The apostle Paul wrote in Romans 13, "The night is far spent, the day [of His coming] is at hand." The last verses of the apocalypse are verses that I always read at a graveside service. "I Jesus have sent mine angel to testify unto you these things in the churches. I am the

156

root and the offspring of David, and the bright and morning star. And the Spirit and the bride say, Come. And let him that hearest say, Come. And let him that is athirst come. And whosoever will, let him take the water of life freely. . . . He which testifieth these things saith, Surely I come quickly." And the answering prayer of the sainted apostle John is, "Amen. Even so, come, Lord Jesus." That is the way we are to live — in expectancy of the soon return of our Savior. So, we can see why the scoffer in Peter's day would ask the question, Where is the promise of His coming?

There is no special sign today of His soon return. "Where is the sign of his coming? for since the fathers fell asleep, all things continue as they were." The sun rises and sets. People marry and they die. Children are born and are reared, and it all continues unabated, unchanged.

GOD'S CLOCK

By inspiration the apostle Peter answers the scoffers in two ways. One of the answers we discussed in our last chapter. "Beloved, be not ignorant of this one thing, that one day is with the Lord as a thousand years, and a thousand years as one day." God's clock is not like our clock and God's time is not like our time. We think the time is long and the Lord delays, when actually He is coming immediately. If by God's clock a thousand years is as a day, then our Savior has not yet been gone two days. And He may come the third day.

GOD'S PROMISE

Another answer the apostle by divine inspiration gives for the delay of our Christ is the fact that "The Lord is not slack concerning his promise." He has not forgotten. He will come back, but He is longsuffering to us — not willing that any should perish, but that all should come to repentance. It is our Lord's prayer that before He comes and visits this earth in judgment, all of us might be saved. It is a tragedy that men take advantage of the longsuffering and merciful goodness of God in order to do evil. For example, in Ecclesiastes 8:11, the wisest man in all the world wrote, "Because sentence against an evil work is not executed speedily, therefore the heart of the sons of men is fully set in them to do evil." If God struck a man down the moment he did wrong, we would be living in an altogether different world. Why does God not strike dead or strike in paralysis or strike with leprosy men who do wrong? The reason is His longsuffering. He hopes, prays, waits, desires that the man will repent and do right before judgment falls upon him. We therefore gain an insight into the heart of God — what God is like. He does not rejoice in the damnation and the cries of agony of those who are lost. Twice in the Bible you will find the Ten Commandments recorded. First, in Exodus 20, when God gave them to Moses. They also are found in Deuteronomy 5 where Moses repeats what God has done. Do you remember how Deuteronomy 5 closes? After Moses names the Ten Commandments and describes the hour when he gave them to the people, he closes with an appeal to the people to obey. This is the heart of the matter — if only people would obey the voice of God.

Ezekiel 33:11 says it this way: "As I live, saith the Lord GOD, I have no pleasure in the death of the wicked; but that the wicked turn from his way and live: turn ye, turn ye from your evil ways; for why will ye die?" That is God — the longsuffering, merciful, kind, heavenly Father. He does not rejoice in condemnation and damnation, and the agony of those who are lost, but pleads with the lost man to turn and be saved. We can find many other illustrations of this pleading in the Bible. They all help us gain an insight into the heart of God. He has no joy in the death of the wicked. And not only that, but He is filled with compassion even to those who curse His name. Even to those who disobey His commandment, God is tender and merciful like a father pleading with a prodigal son or daughter.

GOD'S COMPASSION

I read recently of a professor of homiletics in one of our seminaries. He was teaching his new class of young theologs to preach and he asked each one to read Genesis 3, the story of the Fall and how Adam and Eve hid themselves in the garden when they heard the voice of the Lord in the cool of the day. So each student read the passage to the entire class. One young man stood up and read the passage as though the Lord were a policeman. Another read it as though God were a condemnatory judge, passing sentence. Still another read the passage as though the Lord were indifferent. And another read it as though the Lord were just curious. But then one young man stood up and he read this passage as though God were a broken-hearted Father. "Oh, Adam, where art thou?" When he finished reading it, the professor turned to that young fellow and said, "Young man, you will be a great preacher. You will be a great evangelist, a great soul winner." This young man had caught the true heart of our heavenly Father.

Would you like to know what God is like? Our Savior has said that He who has seen Him has seen the Father. So look at Jesus. What is He like? Do you remember when He asked His disciples who men said He was, and they said many thought Him to be Jeremiah, the weeping prophet? This was because He was at times in tears. One day as He came to the brow of Olivet and looked out over the holy city spread before Him, the Scriptures say He burst into tears. That is the heart of God.

Let me illustrate. This story takes place more than 100 years ago, in the days of the gold and silver rush in the western states. It happened in Silver City, Nevada. A young woman had given her life to be a missionary and in the providence of God was not able to go. Later, she married a man who was the manager of a silver mine in Silver City. In that town, in an adobe hut, lived an old prospector who was dying. He was a vile and loathsome and filthy man. He was evil and cursed so constantly that those who tried to befriend him by bringing him food left it by the bed and went away. This young woman heard about it. She went to that filthy place and looked on the face of that dying prospector. He cursed her, but she, seeking to befriend him, asked, Did you not have a mother who loved you? He cursed his mother for she was also a vile and bad person. The young woman then asked about his wife. The prospector cursed her memory for she was a woman of the streets. Whatever the young woman said was met with an oath and a curse. She left but came back with food the next day and many days after that, but always met those same curses.

One evening, kneeling before bedtime with her children, the young mother was asked by her son if she prayed for the bad man. The mother had to admit she hadn't. The little boy asked, "Mommy, have you given him up?" And his mother had to admit that she had indeed given him up. Then the little boy asked, "But, mommy, has God given him up too?" Then the mother realized God had not given up on him. So she prayed and prayed and prepared to go back.

On her way to that filthy place she met a neighbor and her little girl who said they would go with her. So the three of them went. Again the young woman was met with vile cursing. But while she was there, the little girl playing outside laughed about something. The old man heard this and it sounded like the ringing of a bell. He asked what that was, and when he found out he asked if he could see the girl. The little girl was brought in and in her hand she held a bouquet of purple flowers from the sagebrush. The little girl was frightened but she held out the little bouquet of flowers and the bad man reached forth his bony hand. But he did not touch the flowers. He touched the little dimpled hand of that child and asked her name. The little girl replied that her name was Mamie. Mamie? The old prospector had had a little girl named Mamie, but she had died, and he began to curse God for taking his little girl from him.

However, the young wife saw an opening and inquired about Mamie. Again the miner cursed God for taking her from him. But the young woman spoke to the miner of his mother and wife whom he had cursed and then said, "Sir, it would have been that had your little Mamie been reared by your mother and your wife, she would have grown up to be like them." Well, the vile man had never thought of that. The young woman went on. "Maybe God took your little Mamie that He might keep her pure and fresh for you. And it could be," said the young wife, "that if you would give your heart to Jesus and let Jesus save you, that some day in heaven you could see that darling little girl again." Could it be? The young woman told the man how Jesus had died for his sins that He might wash him, and that He was in heaven waiting for those who love Him, and by His side is a little girl named Mamie. Could Christ forgive someone as bad as he? The man finally repented of his sins and gave his heart to Jesus. But he had never been to church and wanted to go just once. So they decided to bring the church to that hut. All the old prospectors and miners filled that little place and the old man told those inside to get down on their knees for the young woman was going to tell the story of how they could see God some day.

That is God. Whatever is done is always done in pity and tender mercy that God might lead us to trust in Him and to look in faith to Him.

God's Mercy

Lord, why am I not crushed in judgment? Because God is merciful to me. Why does God not visit us in damnation? It is because He is longsuffering. I have never been able to understand how a man could say he would rather choose death than life. Are you that way? Tell me, would you not rather be saved than lost? To be blessed than to be damned? To find everlasting life? That is the good news that in Christ all our sins are washed away. In Him there is hope for heaven now and in the world to come. Answer Him with your life.